Movies, Giant Cookies and a Panther

By

Billy Jack Marsh

Billy Jack Marsh

Copyright © 2008 by Billy Jack Marsh

ISBN: 978-0-615-25725-9

Editor: Mary Fletcher Allderdice Shipp

Copy Editor: Christine Shipp

Book cover designed by:
Marti Marsh

Book text set in True Text Century Gothic,
Text design by MuseScribe
Book design by MFA Shipp
Cover Production by Bob Shipp

<u>Dedication</u>

Movies, Giant Cookies and a Panther

*To my wife Kathleen
and to all our children and
grandchildren*

Billy Jack Marsh

SMILE

As you read through this book, you will laugh on one page, then maybe cry on another. One thing you can be assured of, it was written the way it happened. I, like everyone else who has written a book, owe a lot of thanks to some great people. So . . . to you, the love of my life, Kathy, I love you and thank you much for being my critic. To my children, Janet, Debbie, Donna, Judy and Billy, thanks for the help, but most of all for the smiles and encouragement. And to all my grandchildren, whose love for me and Nana made it easy to write unique stories about them, a special thanks. Special thanks also to Christine, for all her work preparing the story for final editing.

Now . . . read on. Each chapter, large or small, will read like a short story. Each one was written for your enjoyment.

Out, out, brief candle!
Life's but a walking shadow
A poor player, that struts and frets
His hour upon the stage
And then is heard no more.

—William Shakespeare

Movies, Giant Cookies and a Panther

In Alabama in the 1940s, a movie cost ten cents; but best of all were the giant cookies you could buy from the White Star Café. They were delicious and only cost one cent each. They sat on the counter in large glass jars. As you looked at them, your mouth watered.

It was three miles from the movie to our farm in Sibleyville. It was a long walk for a six- and a nine-year-old, but it also gave you plenty of time to eat a bag of giant cookies. It was the best of times.

Especially as Herman, my older brother, would tell of the large panthers that lurked in the woods along the road we were walking. This made us walk faster, as from the dark woods we could almost hear the panthers scream and feel their hot breaths on our legs as we walked faster and faster and faster.

Billy Jack Marsh

ARC Light and Future Glories

My life story could have begun at any point in my lifetime, but ingrained in my memory will always be my first involvement in the Vietnam War. The year was 1965, and although this was not the beginning of my life, it seemed a darn good place to start.

On the far-off Pacific island of Guam, the first of a long line of B-52 bombers had arrived. A decision had been made by the mighty warriors in Washington that the Strategic Air Command would now enter the war.

So it was that the men and machines of this awesome command gathered on Anderson AFB, Guam. There was a feeling of great excitement, as we all felt the North Vietnamese could not stand against the massive bombing which was to take place. The veterans of wars gone by gathered in the clubs at night and as the brew took effect, many yarns were spun of their past glories. As they talked, you could almost hear the engines of the old B-29s come to life on Tinnian Island, as they prepared for take off to bomb Japan in World War II.

The younger men, like me, would listen in awe and dream of our future glories, which would surely come now the big bombers, were readied for the beginning. The date was June 13, 1965. As I said before, this was not the beginning. My life's story really began in a small town in Alabama; the year was 1931.

December 30ᵗʰ, 1931:
The Day I Was Born

My mom was very fortunate that Dr. McCarn was available on the night I was born. He arrived at our house only a short time before I was ready to enter this world. He looked at my dad and said, "Gus, get a tub of hot water ready. Also, take another tub and put snow in it, add some water. Your baby is coming into this world feet-first. Your wife really needs to be in the hospital, but we don't have time. We may lose the baby. It doesn't look good."

The birth took more than thirty minutes. I had been smothered and was not breathing. Doctor McCarn put me in the hot tub first, then into the ice cold water. When I came out of the ice water, they said I let out a scream. That's how the fifth child arrived in the Marsh household.

Three years later, we would move to a place named Burton Hill. We would live there for only one year, and then move to Warrior. My dad, a coal miner, would go to work at Kings Coal Mine. He worked a ten-hour day and made 55 cents a day and was lucky to get that. They didn't pay you actual money. They gave you tokens that you could spend in their commissary. That way, they could cheat you twice. These people were professional crooks. This would all end about five years later when World War II came.

One Man, Two Names

When I was born in Trafford, Alabama in 1931, there was a discussion as to what I would be named. A Mrs. Page who lived near us wanted to name me Billy Jack, while my Dad wanted to name me after one of his brothers, Robert Milton. The discussion was never resolved as to what I was to be called, until after Dr. McCarn (who signed the birth certificate) had departed from our home, where I was born. Little did we know the problem this caused years later.

I had always used the name Billy Jack, but now as I was eighteen years old, I had decided to join the Air Force. I left home early that morning on a bus to Birmingham. After taking an I.Q. test and being examined by doctors, it was now time to be sworn into the Air Force. But before this, they would need to check each person's birth certificate to be sure each of us was at least 18 years old. I and several other people didn't have the certificate. The recruiter said he would go to the county health department, which was only two blocks away, and get the birth records. When he returned, he said to me, "There's a James, a Herman, and a Ray; also a Robert Milton — which one is you?" Thank goodness, I remembered my mom told me I was almost named Robert Milton. When I explained I had never used this name, he said, "O.K., your name is Billy Jack. Don't ever use the name Robert Milton."

So I entered the Air Force as Billy Jack Marsh. I had a sworn statement from my Mom that I always carried with me, which stated Billy Jack and Robert Milton were one and the same person. So today, 58 years later, I still remain the man with two names. I don't guess it really matters after all this time.

Poverty
Warrior, Alabama — 1936

Standing on the side of the road thumbing a ride, I was five years old and had decided to escape this poverty I lived in. My friend Pookey Russell, also five, was on one side of US Highway 31 thumbing one way while I was thumbing a ride the other way. The police officer of this small town came by and carried us home. He told my mom to keep us off the highway or we might get killed. My mom wasn't happy; she would soon be very mad.

That night, Pookey and I sneaked out of our houses and went to the railway yard switching spur, and climbed into a boxcar. This boxcar was hooked to a train bound for Mobile, Alabama, and that was where they found us — one hundred and fifty miles from home. We were sent back by bus, and after some severe talking-to, we decided to give up travel for a while, until maybe we were six or seven years old. My mom was really concerned, while my dad saw the humor in all this.

A year later, we would leave Warrior and move to a place called Coaldale. There, we were in the country with plenty of hills and trees to climb. We also had a creek to swim in and fish. It wasn't much better than where we lived before, but at least everyone who lived here was about the same. We were all in the same boat — poor as dirt.

My brother, James, was the oldest. He would work any job to make a little money. He would carry stacks of barrel staves miles for this company and would come home at night exhausted. When he reached 17, he started to work in a coalmine. He was one year too young, but they would hide him when the mine inspectors were around.

When James met Dorothy White and fell madly in love, we noticed he had bought himself some new shirts and jeans, also a nice hair comb, toothbrush and toothpaste. We were warned — "keep your hands off my stuff". He wasn't mean; he just wanted to be Mister Right for Dorothy. After seeing her one day, I didn't blame him: she was beautiful, and had a great personality. One day, I wore one of his shirts to school. It was the day pictures were made. The shirt was too big, but was better than anything I had. He was a real unhappy guy, when he found out what I had done.

My brother Herman, a few years older than I, continued in school until age 16. Then he went to work. In a few years, he found a job working at Drennen Motor Company, and soon became a "Class A" mechanic. He then lived near Birmingham. He would come back home some weekends and always brought us two younger kids something.

As for my two older sisters — one would continue in school and graduate, she was the youngest. Doris would meet John Jolly and a few years later they were married. John was in the Army Air Force and they had a pretty good life. Gussie, the oldest sister, married William Nichols. He drove busses for Birmingham Transit Corporation.

We were now about to enter a war. I was eleven years old. Ray, my youngest brother, was seven. We were the last ones left at home. We moved to Sibleyville in 1941. That year, the war would start.

Out of Food—Out of Hope

In 1937, I was six years old and we were living in Warrior, Alabama. My Dad, who was a coal miner, was working for Kings Coal Mining Company. He made the grand total of 55 cents a day. One night, while he was away, we completely ran out of food. My Mom, bless her, was frantic. We were literally on the brink of starvation. I remember the only thing we had in the house to eat was a small bag of cornmeal. She placed this on a sheet pan, put it in the oven of our wood burning stove and parched it, then set on the table. We kids sat eating the corn meal and drinking water.

The next day, my Dad came home. He had met a black man who had worked at a coal mine a few years before and was now sharecropping an old farm about a mile out of Warrior. He told my Dad he had plenty of vegetables and also he had a group of Indian plum trees, apples and pears. We kids set around eating the fruit until we were about to pop. My Dad and this old black man dug up Irish and sweet potatoes. Then they set out to picking beans, peas, corn, tomatoes and anything else had in this large garden. We kids played marbles in the dirt in the front yard. It was a great day.

Strange, with all the hatred between whites and blacks back then it never entered my mind that I was playing games with someone I wasn't supposed to. Afterwards, we gathered up all this food in large potato sacks and they walked home with us carrying all this food. We had a two-week supply of everything. A week later, this same black man came to our house. He had a large bag and inside was a pork shoulder and a piece of seasoning pork. He said, "Thought you might like this."

I was only six years old but I remember this like it was yesterday. As the old black man walked away down the road, I remember he had a little skip in his walk, like he had done something great —and he had!

These were desperate times, but they would get better in about four years. But my Mom and Dad were still to face these years not knowing what the future held in store for them. Coaldale, the floods and all the other adventures would follow. Life would be hard but we would survive.

Vinide

When I was about seven years old my friend, Russell, was sent to Mr. Lane's store that had recently opened about a mile from our house at Coaldale. He was supposed to buy a gallon of vinegar as his mother was pickling cucumbers. Arriving at the store, he proceeded to ask for a gallon of "vinide," pronounced vin-i-de. He just could not say "vinegar". Everyone in the store started to laugh. After being asked several times what he wanted, he became so embarrassed, he blurted out, "I need a gallon of kerosene." He took it home. His mother was furious, but, needless to say, she never sent him to a store after vinegar again.

A few days later, my mom had given me the first dollar I had ever had to take to the store; when I entered Mr. Lane's store, several men were sitting around having one of their country store conversations. They knew Russell was my friend. The first thing that was said to me was, "Hey, Billy, you come to get your friends vinide?" I wasn't too happy about how they were acting. I turned to one of them and said, "No, I'm really here to buy a gallon of kerosene so I can pour it on you." You didn't say those types of things to a grownup back during those years. I thought he would tell my Dad and I would be punished for my smart mouth, but nothing was ever said to my Dad. I guess this man thought what he said wasn't too nice to a seven-year-old.

Ten Years Old and Full of Mischief

When I was about ten years old, one of our favorite things was to go bird thrashing. You may be wondering what that is. We would take a carbide lamp (like miners used), shine the light into the bushes at night, and find birds that were roosting there, shoot them with a slingshot, skin them out and roast them over a fire. We really thought we were being great hunters. When you're poor, any food tastes good, and these birds were quite tasty. Sometimes we would get ourselves a rabbit. Then the feast was on. I look back now at all the things I did when I was a kid, a lot of it was funny, but also a lot of it was dangerous. I guess when you're young, things just don't seem as bad as they are and maybe, just maybe, that's a good thing.

But because I loved to hunt and roam the woods, there were several times I placed my life in danger.

One year, while hunting for pine knots, which were removed from rotted pinewood and used to start fires in our fireplace and our wood stove, I sensed someone was watching me. I stopped chopping the wood knots out of a log and then I thought I could hear something breathing. I slowly turned around and there, setting on a log not more than twenty yards from me, was mountain lion. He was lying on the log, not moving at all. I knew if I ran he would naturally think I was prey and attack. There was a stump a few feet away, so I sat down with my axe and just stared back at this big cat. I said to myself, *if he attacks, I'll use this stump as a shield while I fight him with my axe.* But thank goodness, after a short while, he lost interest and walked away. I never went back into those woods again without my brother and a shotgun.

Coaldale, Alabama 1938-1940
Poor as Dirt, but Happy

We all have a tendency to make things worse than they really were. But, during my childhood, we literally had nothing. We were not alone, as almost all the families in our area were the same or worse. When I tell my children we were still going to school barefooted at the age of eleven, they look at me with much doubt. You may be laughing now, but poverty is tough. But somehow you survive, and because of this you are a better person. For several years I felt I was inferior to other kids my age. When I reached 15 years old things changed. I was now admired by my peers, but even at this age, we were a poor family. About this time, I would start thinking about joining the Air Force. I knew a better life awaited me.

But before this would happen, I would go through a learning process over the next three years. I would learn what girls were all about, but because I was just plain shy, girls would make my life miserable at times. I remember my brother Herman taking me with him on a double date to a drive-in movie. The girl must have though I was plain weird. She kept trying to kiss me, but I kept fighting her off. She finally asked me if I disliked her, but I said, "No, but kissing is a bad way to spread a cold." She started to laugh. Then she just had to tell her girlfriend what I had said and I was so embarassed I must have turned purple. After a stern briefing by my brother, I tried to be more friendly on my next date with this girl.

1941: World War II

In 1941, I was ten years old. I did not understand what had happened, but my Dad said the Japanese had attacked Pearl Harbor and now we would go to war. He tried to enlist in the military, but they told him he was past the age they were accepting. When Germany declared war on us, he would try again and receive the same answer. It was at least a year before I knew what this war was all about.

As word spread about what the enemy was doing to our soldiers in the Pacific, the whole country was filled with rage and ready to fight. When the war ended, I was fifteen years old. Many young men just eight years older than me entered the military. Several died and this caused great sadness, not only in the school, but throughout our community and the town of Warrior. Shortly after the war, my brother James entered the Navy and was assigned to the SeaBees. When the island of Okinawa was invaded, he helped build and repair the runways for what would be our forward bases to bomb Japan. He told us after he returned home how dangerous it was working out in the open. Many times men were hit by sniper fire. He was a good brother and a good man, but he died very young, as you will see later in this book.

It was almost like a lifetime had passed. We were living on a farm in Sibleyville, Alabama. I remember we celebrated the war's end by making homemade ice cream. My oldest sisters came home from the munitions factory in Birmingham and we all had a great time. I would go to school at Warrior for another year, then we moved, and our lives changed forever.

Gun Battle on the Street in Warrior

It was Saturday morning; we had come to Warrior, a small town three miles from Coaldale, where we lived. We first went to Mr. Ogletree's Grocery Store. After buying a few items, we went up the street to the drug store. My Dad wanted to buy us a fountain coke. We had just got our drinks when we heard shouting outside; we went to the window and looked out.

A man was standing against a car with a gun in his hand. Another man was coming around the other side of the car. (We didn't know it then, but this second man was the sheriff of Warrior.) All of a sudden, the man with the pistol started shooting the second man, the sheriff. The pistol was a small caliber gun called a Lemon Squeezer, so named because it had no trigger and fired when the pistol grip was squeezed. The sheriff fell against the car, and then slowly walked around it, supporting himself by leaning against it. He pulled his .38 Police Special from his holster, took aim, fired one shot and killed the gunman. He then fell dead himself. I must have been about ten years old. I can still see this happening as though it was yesterday.

The sight of this happening would stay with me for a long time. But on the way home, my Dad would explain to me that things happen. He would always say to me, "Billy, there are a lot of things we cannot change and cannot understand. Sometimes you just smile and move on." He winked at me and said, "Remember we are the best." I believe deep in his heart and mind he felt that was very true.

The Sailor Who Learned To Fly — 1940s

Saturday was the day when all the country people would go to town. My dad took me along one time. The trip was to buy food for the next week, although we bought very little, as most of our food came from the farm we lived on. After gathering what we were to buy, we started to walk up the street heading out of town. My dad stopped in front of the town saloon and said to me, "Sit here on the bench, I'll be back out soon."

Shortly after he entered the saloon, a sailor walked up and went inside.

In a few seconds, I heard loud voices inside, and suddenly the sailor came flying through the plate glass window, out of the saloon. A man came out and said, "Guess your dad didn't like being called an S.O.B." The man said my dad had grabbed the sailor by the collar and seat of the pants and threw him out of the bar while exclaiming, "You're a disgrace to your uniform." My dad, having been a hero in the Battle of the Argonne Forest during World War I, couldn't stand anyone who didn't respect our country. He was one-of-a-kind and loved by all who knew him.

Widows Cry When Mean Men Die — Coaldale 1943

His name was Buck Slatton and he was one mean fellow. One day, I heard all this shouting on the road that ran in front of our house. I looked around the corner of the house. There on the road was some man wearing a woman's dress. He had a shotgun and was threatening everyone he saw. A woman who lived in the house next door was sitting in a rocking chair on her porch. He threatened to shoot her if she stopped rocking. He left there, and the next day we found out he had gone to a man's house to collect moonshine money owed him. The man who supposedly owed him this money waited for him behind a large pine tree and when Buck was close, stepped out and shot him dead.

I went to his brother's house the next day. He was being buried in a half suit they used in those days. One of the men pulled back the suit so I could see the bullet holes. I remember he said to me, "The world's a better place without him." As mean as he was, I guess he was right.

A Mean Man — 1940s

We didn't know he was in the house, although this was normal in rural Alabama in the 1940s. Now a man stood at our kitchen table. Herman, my next-to-oldest brother, Ray, the youngest, our mom and I had just sat down to eat.

This man spoke in an unfriendly tone, "Where is your brother James?" Herman looked up, and called him by name, "Buck, what do you need with him?" Buck Slaton answered, "Don't give me any backtalk! Now, where is he?" Our mom, who sensed trouble, looked up. "Buck, he's at the coalmine off Trafford Road." Buck Slaton left in a hurry. We had all noticed that he had kept his right hand at his waist, inside his shirt. We realized that he might have a gun.

Mom looked at Herman, her voice quivering, "Herman, cut across the valley. The coalmine is only one mile over the next hill; if you hurry, you might beat him to the mine."

Herman arrived at the mine just seconds before Buck showed up. James was working with Lester Slaton, Buck's brother. When Lester heard the news, he told James, "Leave right now! My brother Buck is a mean man!" James and Herman left for home. When they arrived, they found our dad had gotten home from work, and had loaded the double-barreled 12-gauge shotgun. Dad had also gone up the road to tell Mitchell Slaton, a good friend of his who happened to be Buck's older brother, "If he comes back to our house, I will not hesitate to use this shotgun."

This whole incident came about because James and his wife, Dorothy, had done Buck Slaton a favor by taking his four-year-old daughter to an all-day singing and dinner on the grounds, an event that churches regularly held in those days. Now this kindness had backfired, due to James having made an off-the-cuff remark during the day that he would never again take this spoilt brat to any church function. This statement had then been related to Buck Slaton by a drunk Buck had met in a bar in Warrior. Now, after having drunk most of the day away, Buck was going to make James pay for his insult.

Buck stood on our porch; Dad told him to leave immediately. Buck threatened to kill both Dad and James. "Now," said our dad, "You are about to die. James, open the door." James said, "Dad, wait another minute!" A different voice could be heard outside, telling Buck to leave. It was his brother Mitchell, saying, "Mr. Marsh will not discuss this. If he opens that door, you will die."

There was silence out on the porch, then the sound of a car door slamming. We heard a car engine start up, and they were gone.

The Flood

In 1943, after many days of rain, the little Warrior River became flooded. Because of this, the creek that flowed through our community jumped its banks and started to flood the valley where we lived. My dad and mom were worried sick that the house would be covered with water, and to complicate their feelings, my brothers and I ran around hollering, "The flood is coming and we are all going to die!" We watched the water rise all day; that night we moved all our household goods to a hill nearby.

The next morning, we awoke with the sun shining and all the homes in the valley were completely covered with water. Not even the roofs were visible. It stayed that way for about 24 hours and slowly started to recede. Many homes were washed from their foundations, but our home settled back on its foundation. After a day of cleaning the house, we moved back into our home.

In 1944, we moved to an old farm a few miles from Coaldale. It was there that my Uncle Bill came to live with us. This land was as fertile as any I have ever seen. Nothing had been planted here for years. That first summer, we planted a large garden. We had enough vegetables for not only ourselves but for anyone who wanted them as well, and there were many people who came forward and accepted this offer. We also planted a large watermelon and cantaloupe patch. On the 4th of July that first year, we held a little southern ceremony and cut the first of these melons.

The farmhouse we lived in was very old and had been made of rough lumber. There was a large front porch and three rooms downstairs. I will never forget the large stone fireplace in the living room, for there in front of the fire we spent many a winter night as my dad and mom told us the story of their lives. A large set of stairs led to a loft and that is where my brothers and I spent our hours of sleep. We weren't all that dumb, for in the winter months all the heat came upstairs with us. The following year, we planted about 25 acres of corn and cotton. This I remember very well, for we had all agreed once we had decided to plant this crop, we must all help out to the finish of harvest.

The "Model A" Truck

It's hard to believe all the things that would occur in fifteen years as I first lived in a place called Burton Hill, then Coaldale, then on to Warrior. From there I would return to Coaldale, then to Sibleyville and finally to Gardendale, just outside Birmingham. I had taught myself to drive by the time I was eleven years old. I would drive my mom and my Aunt Pearl from Coaldale to Gardendale, which was about twelve miles.

The vehicle was a Model A Ford made in 1931. The body had been cut down and made into a wooden-bed truck. The worst thing about these vehicles was that they had mechanical brakes and had to be adjusted every 20 miles. Failure to do this could render the brakes useless. It wasn't too bad on level ground, but in those Alabama hills, you'd better have brakes.

I loved that old truck. My dad couldn't get a license because he couldn't read, so I drove him wherever he wanted to go. One day, my dad let a cousin of our family drive the truck. He wrecked it and almost killed himself, my brother and my dad. We could never afford another vehicle again. I had horses to ride anywhere I wanted to go, but that didn't help the family. It was a sad day, losing our truck.

The Race

In the late 1940s, my Uncle Bill came to visit us in Coaldale, Alabama, and as usual, he had traveled by wagon, with a small string of horses following along behind. One horse was different than all the other horses, a black mare that stood more than 17 hands tall and was gifted with great intelligence for a horse. Junior Hill, who owned a stallion that was extremely fast, was persistent on holding a race between his horse and the black mare. The race, if run, would be on an unpaved road that ran by our house, a straight about three quarters of a mile long. My uncle told him his horse could not beat this black mare. Junior insisted the race would be winner-take-all. Finally, my uncle agreed to the race.

When we lined up to race, I noticed the black mare became very intense and quivered with anticipation. The signal was given to start. She lunged forward so quickly, I almost slipped off, as I was riding bare-back. Within fifty yards, we led by five lengths. Then, she lengthened her stride and pulled away.

My uncle took Junior's horse, kept it overnight, and then gave it back to him. We would move to the farm at Sibleyville a few months later.

Nail Meets Foot — 1943

We had lived along Coaldale Creek for about seven years. Now we had moved to Sibleyville just two miles away. The same creek wandered behind our house. That was a real plus during the hot summers in Alabama. But this was not the time of the year to use the creek for swimming. It was early November, and that meant hog-slaughtering season.

Two days before we had slaughtered the hog, water was boiled in a large cast iron pot, and then placed in a 55-gallon drum buried at an angle in the ground. The hog was placed in the drum, and then pulled out with a lot of hand rubbing. This removed the hair.

We ate most every part of that hog — the head, brains, the skin—we would have eaten the pig's last squeal if we could have caught it. Times were really tough, and for me it was about to get even worse.

We had burned some old wood to heat the water in the cast iron pot. Now, two days later, I ran bare-footed through the pile of cold ashes. As I did, I felt this very sharp pain in my right foot. I went down heavy. When I sat up, I was amazed to see a very large nail protruding through the top of my foot. It was just back of where the toes join the foot, and wedged between the bones.

I needed help, but my mom was the only one home. I didn't want to frighten her. I pulled my foot into my lap. I knew I was in deep trouble when I pulled on the nail and it refused to come out. Also, I noticed I became dizzy when I pulled on the nail. I was not a happy little boy. I was only twelve years old. I sat there thinking.

Finally, I reached at the sole of my foot, placed the head of the nail snugly against the hand between my fingers, squeezed tightly, closed my eyes, took a deep breath and pulled the nail and it slipped out of my foot. I lay on the ground, shaking. I finally made my way to the back porch and called my mom. She couldn't believe I hadn't called her before. She washed my foot, then took a gallon kerosene can, placed the nozzle over the puncture wound, and let the fluid flow through the hole. Finally, she wrapped my foot with clean cloth. A few days later, I was back to normal. That was about 1943. How tough were we then?? Real tough!

The Laboratory 1941-1943

I always fancied myself as a scientist and doctor, so when a boy came to play with us one day, I had a chance to practice on him, as he had a deep infection in one of his legs. I told him I could make up some ointment in my laboratory that would heal his sore.

As I remember now, the mixture was made of carbide dust after water was used to activate the carbide (to make light in a carbide lamp), cow feed, kerosene, and black pepper. His mom almost had a heart attack when she found what we did. But, lo and behold! It worked, and his sore was healed.

The laboratory was really a storm pit or tornado shelter dug into a bank near our house and covered with logs, tin roofing and dirt. My brother, Herman, almost blew himself up messing with all my secret laboratory chemicals like cow feed, kerosene and nail polish. How did I survive, myself?— I really don't know.

A Trooper, a Side Seat Driver, and My Dad

As we came around the curve on this little dirt road, I was shocked to see a state trooper's black and white car parked across the railroad train bed that led to our farmhouse in Sibleyville. It was 1943, and I was twelve years old. I knew I was in deep trouble. I was four years too young for a driver's license, and sitting in the right seat was my brother, Ray, also known as Cooter. He was about eight years old.

The troopers had stopped some men with moonshine and were in the process of emptying all the jugs. One of the troopers looked at us and then asked why water was spitting out of a seam on the engine. In my attempt to tell him that a piece of the head gasket had blown out, I actually said a piece of the driver license had blown out.

He smiled and then asked Ray if he was the backseat driver. Ray replied, "No, I'm the side seat driver." They followed us up the train bed to our house. Then they told my dad not to let me drive until I was 16 years old. My dad's reply was, "I'll try not to let him get caught again." The trooper looked at my dad and said, "Mr. Marsh, understand— he can't drive. He's too young." Then he left. I did thank him. The next day I was back driving. No one else knew. I was just a lot more careful where I went.

Honesty

My brother, Herman, loved to hunt. During World War II, everything was on ration, including munitions of any kind. One day, Herman came home from school with two shotgun shells and was bragging that he was going to go hunting on the weekend. My dad asked where he got the shells. Herman was a little vague about this. My dad now asked in a more forcible way. Finally, he admitted he had stolen the shells from the hardware store in Warrior, a town three miles away, but near our school. My dad had come in from working a ten-hour day in a coalmine, but this did not stop him from marching Herman three miles to Warrior to go to the hardware store owner's house, return the shells and apologize. My dad was furious. Honesty was everything to him.

I'm sure a large part of his obsession with being honest was because of his lack of money and everyday necessities of life. He had gone to work in a coal mine when he was twelve years old. He was the only support for his family. Later in life, he would share anything he had with others. I remember well, if anyone stopped at our house, no matter what time of the night, he would get up and cook them something to eat. It was something people who were kind during the depression years would do for others, and my Dad was a very kind man. He shared his love of life with all those around him. I always felt he used up a lot of his life helping others. When I look back now, I realize that he was the best of the best. He passed this on to all his children and in turn, his grandchildren, and great grandchildren.

The Wagon and Me — 1943

I was lying in the road. I couldn't breathe. The last thing I remembered was the wagon wheel missing my head by inches. I had fallen between the brake and the left rear wheel. I could see my dad's face above me. Then, I heard him say, "He's not breathing." My lungs had been deflated by the wagon wheel, which had passed over my chest. He picked me up by my pants' waistband and then dropped me flat on my back. Air re-entered my lungs and I started to breath. My dad said, "Billy, I told you to leave that brake handle alone."

On a wagon, a large pad connected to a pole would scrub against a wheel when a rope attached to it was pulled by the driver or passenger, which would slowly stop the wagon. This wagon was loaded with corn and was very heavy, and was being pulled by two horses.

I could have died very easily, but we were raised so rough during those days, you didn't die very easily. But, after this incident, I now had a healthy respect for horse-pulled wagons.

Warrior, Alabama and Other Places

How would you like to live in a place named Peep Crack? You won't find too many places in the USA with that name. What about the name Flea Holler? Strange — but I lived there. A dirt road ran in front of our house and just over the road was a small creek. That was where we got our water to wash our clothes. You could also bathe there in the summer.

We went to church at a place called Scratch Out. Try to figure that one out. How it got that name, I never knew. It was the Church of God back during these years. It was still there, when I visited there recently. My oldest brother, James, is also buried there. A place called Nyota is only two miles form there, and as you travel there you pass Dade's Hill.

One mile north of Flea Holler, and in the bend of the road where you left Coaldale Road to go to Scratch Out, a store once stood. It was owned and run by a blind man, and was therefore known as the Blind Man's store. Can you imagine that today? As it's sometimes said, "They would have robbed him blind." There were other places like Corner — corner of what? Cane Creek: must have been a creek with lots of cane crowing nearby. Strange names, but no stranger than my life.

Yes, I was a little boy in a world I didn't understand, but somehow I survived. Read on, for in these stories and in this book, you will find many short stories about life, and ninety-eight percent is exactly as it happened. The places listed above were where I lived, or places I went to, during my childhood. Life was much simpler during this time. I am sure you will find no new places with names like this today.

I loved my life the way it was during the 1930s and late 1940s. It was all I could ever want, even if it was tough — but I can assure you, it made me a better person. Most of these years, you survived by your wits. You really had one choice, be smart in every thing you did, otherwise you would not survive in a time of poverty and despair. When I look back now, I realize it was a time when love for each other was what carried us through desperate times.

The Fish That Came To Dinner —1946

"Wake up, we just caught a fish five feet long!" We were all camping out on the Warrior River and had set out trot lines. This was a way of fishing where you string a line across the river, placing hooks and weights about every five feet. You bait the hooks, and come back to check these lines about every three hours. Sometimes you catch lots of fish, sometimes nothing. This time we had gotten off to a good start.

They held this giant fish up next to me, its tail on the ground and its head above me. It was almost five feet long. My dad was so happy he almost couldn't talk. We decided to clean and roast the fish, even though it was about 10 o'clock at night. Someone said they wished we had some corn to roast, as it sure would go well with the fish. Then it was remembered a cornfield was just up stream from our camp.

James and Herman took the boat and were soon back with two-dozen ears of corn. The round green things they also were carrying weren't corn, though. The farmer must have known we were going to be there — he had planted watermelons in the corn patch so we would have dessert!

It was one great time, and we all fell asleep about two o'clock in the morning. When I woke up, the sun was shining through the trees, and Dad had come back from running the trot lines and started cooking breakfast: salt pork, eggs, coffee, and sliced white bread. All this and his great big smile — I couldn't ask for more.

The Legend of Lost Lake

The one thing my dad really enjoyed was fishing. Every spring, we would always go to the Tennessee River. We fished mostly the backwaters that had overflowed during heavy rains over the years.

One of his favorite places to fish for crappie was a place called Lost Lake. He loved to catch crappie. They had a lot of fight for their size, usually under a pound. In addition, the fish was one of our favorites to eat. My dad would sit in the boat with a big smile on his face, relating stories about all the fishing trips he and his son-in-laws had been on. He'd reminisce about camping out on the ground, sitting around a campfire drinking coffee, then fixing their breakfast the next morning, all the time saying, "hurry up, the fish are hungry too". He made the trip very interesting, to say the least.

In 1942, we made a trip to Lost Lake, close to Athens, Alabama and not far from the Tennessee line. We arrived about seven o'clock in the morning and were soon fishing. We caught about twenty crappie in the first two hours, before they slacked off biting. We sat there in the sun, and my dad started telling about the old days. Finally, he said, "Billy, you like this lake?" I said it was nice, and added, "how did it get its name?"

Dad related how there was a small town here once, and the Tennessee River flooded and covered the town; some people had lost their lives. The town is still down there. Sometimes when the water is rough, the church bell in the church steeple rings, and if you listen carefully, you can hear it.

I sat there, thinking about this town and the people who lived here. I looked over the side of the boat. Was there really a town down there? I looked up at my dad's face. He was smiling. I was only eleven years old in 1942, and he was my hero, and I loved him very much.

An Old Horse and a .32 Caliber Pistol

"I sure would like to buy your horse." I looked up. I recognized the voice. I said, "Hi, Junior. Naw, you don't want that old plug. He's pretty old, you know. His teeth aren't too sound." He looked at me, "I really would like to have the horse." I said, "Junior, he's been chewing grass, then spitting out the husk and swallowing the juice. He's really skinny." He insisted, and I finally said okay. "What will you give for the horse?" He said, "I've got a thirty-two Smith and Wesson pistol I'll trade you for the horse." I agreed. I made this trade at the age of twelve. I now owned a pistol.

I cautioned Junior not to give this horse much corn, as the horse could swell up, not being used to eating it. He took the horse home and gave the horse too much corn. With his bad teeth being unable to chew the feed properly, the corn swelled up in the horse's stomach. He promptly became bloated, laid down, and died that very night.

The next day, Junior saw me, and said, "Billy, you knew that horse would die." I couldn't help but laugh, even though I felt bad that the horse had suffered. I still have the gun sixty-two years later; it will be passed on to one of the family. The story will live on in this book and someone will read it and smile.

My Mom, Aunt Pearl
And the Model A Truck

One morning my Aunt Pearl came to our house. It was about a mile from their farm that was set on top of a hill that overlooked the valley where we lived. She always had a smile on her face. She dipped snuff—a certain brand named Bruton, and in the corner of her mouth you could see a small brown wet residue from her snuff. There was always a spit can nearby and she would sit there, spitting, talking and laughing with my mom, who also dipped snuff. I didn't understand what enjoyment was derived from this habit, but I was only twelve years old at this time.

Gardendale was twelve miles from Warrior, and it was three miles to Warrior from our farm at Sibleyville. They had asked me if I could drive to my sister Doris' house at Gardendale. I said sure, so we climbed into this 1931 Model A Ford that had half of the body cut off and made into a wooden-bed truck. It was a tight fit in the cab with three people, although at the time I only weighed about one hundred ten pounds.

The only thing I was worried about was that about half way we had to climb a twisting mountain road known as Horse Branch Hill. It was very steep, and the truck had very limited power. It really was scary, especially with mechanical brakes, and those on the rear wheels only. I crawled under the car and adjusted the brakes prior to leaving.

The drive was only about an hour. Our top speed was only about twenty-five miles an hour. We stayed all day at my sister's. She cooked us a nice meal and a great cake. She also had cakes from a bakery where John, her husband, worked. When we loaded up to leave we took some of these cakes and cinnamon rolls to our house for the rest of the family.

We started home. I was really worried about the ride down Horse Branch Hill. By gearing down the transmission, our speed never passed twenty-five miles an hour. Still, I was very scared, and had used up most of my brake adjustment; we still had a long twisting road that was steep down off Coaldale Hill. In thirty minutes we approached the hill. I knew it could be an adventure to the bottom. Did we make it??? Well, I'll just say I'm writing this story and my Aunt Pearl died of natural causes, a long time later. My mom lived on to 1990. But, if they were still here today, they would be laughing, and unlike my mom, who quit snuff a few years before she died, Aunt Pearl would still be dipping and spitting.

Six Bullets, a Pig,
A Sledge Hammer and a Funny Man
1946 – Sibleyville

It was time to slaughter the pig. Fall of the year had come and we would smoke the hams and make the salt pork for seasoning, but before that would come the ritual where pork chops were cut off the pig and cooked while the meat was still warm.

We had started to kill the pig an hour before this. My dad took the .32 Smith and

Wesson revolver that belonged to me, even though I was only 14 years old. He took aim and fired two feet away from the pig's head. The pig didn't stop eating the corn placed in the trough to keep him still during this ordeal. My dad pulled back the hammer and fired again. Same result. It was now obvious this pig had one hard head. After he had shot this pig five times and he wouldn't stop eating, my dad was now mad. Grabbing a sledgehammer, he hit the pig in the head, trying to knock it unconscious. The pig now ran around and around the pen with my dad chasing it and swinging the sledgehammer, and I might add, saying some words that you won't hear in church.

After about a half hour of this, Dad finally had to take a break. He was covered with sweat and mud from the pigpen and smelled awful. I went into the house, got six more bullets for the gun, loaded it, came back, and fired one shot and the pig pitched forward dead. We now cleaned the hair off the pig by submerging him in boiling water and scraping the hair off.

My dad exclaimed several times my gun only worked right when I was firing it. We laughed for years about how funny it was on that day. I know I will never forget how funny he looked chasing that pig with a 10-pound sledgehammer. He was one of a kind, and he was my dad.

The Farmhouse at Sibleyville, 1943-1947

This was the place I would grow from a small boy to a teenage semi-man. To say that this was a place of hard work would only be a half truth. Many times, we built a small dam across a creek that ran nearby. This would serve as the swimming hole during the long hot summers when water became scarce. The bottom land along the creek was where we planted corn in the rich soil. Corn stalks were ten feet high and would put on five or six ears of corn per stalk. All the other land served for cotton, vegetables, watermelons, and cantaloupes. We had all the vegetables we could possibly eat.

My Uncle Bill was a horse trader, and when you saw him coming, he always had a string of horses behind his wagon. We kids loved to race each other on his horses.

The old farmhouse had a loft with stairs from the floor below. This was where I slept. It had a tin roof and was great when it rained. Some of our most happy days were spent here; I know my dad loved this place. It was pretty nice when your fishing hole was only fifty yards from your back porch.

When we left there in 1948, it was sad, but we were moving near Birmingham, a place named Gardendale. There we would live happily with our sister Doris and brother-in-law, John, until I left for the Air Force, and my dad would die — things had changed, and would never be the same.

President Roosevelt Dies & World War II Ends

I spent most of my afternoons plowing the fields. Many a night, I was in the field until after nine o'clock. This old farm was located about two miles from the nearest main road. I ran those two miles every day to catch my school bus. This distance is really open to conjecture by my children, after seeing where I lived. They say it really wasn't that far. When I took the kids to visit the old homestead a few years ago, only the old cistern still stood, but as I stood there, all my childhood days flashed before my eyes again, and I am sure if you had listened really closely, you could have heard my Dad's rumbling voice as he called us into the old farm house.

In 1945, a great president died, and I can still remember my uncle and aunt coming to our house to tell us the news. They were full of grief, for these poor and lonely people loved this president, and they felt as though a dear friend had died. Shortly thereafter, the atomic bomb would explode over Hiroshima and Nagasaki and World War II would suddenly end. I remember, we all gathered at our home on that historic day.

My sisters, who lived in Birmingham, were there, and for this festive occasion, we celebrated with homemade ice cream.

The next year, my Uncle Bill went back to his horse-trading and I became a super-jock in high school. I was a good athlete, and would try any game. I had been toughened by the years on the farm and possessed good speed and strength. Although 140 pounds, I lashed many balls out of Warrior Stadium in the next two years. And though short for basketball, as a guard I used my speed to good use. I always said, if you can't out-jump them, then you can always drive by them.

In football, my first year, I played guard. I really loved the contact. Using the old Notre Dame Box Formation, the guards pulled out to block on every play. I loved every minute of it, for there was no greater thrill than to lay a linebacker flat with a body block. My second and third years, I played halfback. There I excelled. We had a great team during this time. They said it was the best the school had ever had.

Warrior High School, 1945

When we left sixth grade, we moved to a red brick building across the road. This was called high school, even though it was the seventh grade. Since I would play football as per direction of Mr. Self, the principal, I would go to class with thirty-six girls for Homeroom, Math, Science and History. This was so I could fit all my classes into a day prior to one o'clock, as that was when football practice started, and also because I had to catch the bus home at three o'clock. The reason the rest of the class was all girls was because when we left sixth grade to go to seventh grade (high school), our class of 72 students was divided into two—36 boys and 36 girls.

One day while in class, the teacher had gone to the principal's office, and all the girls were really up to a lot of mischief. The teacher walked in, she just stood looking at us, and then declared, "Line up in front of my desk." Little did I know what she had on her mind.

From her desk, she pulled out a paddle made from a thick board, and as I was first in line, she proceeded to bend my hand back and whacked across it with great vigor. My hand was on fire; all the girls smiled as they looked at me. To say I was embarrassed doesn't cover how I felt.

Later, I would receive notes passed up to me saying things like they would kiss my hand better, and I would turn red with embarrassment. Still later, things would get worse, or so I thought.(OR: I thought that things could only get worse from there on out.) In a few years, these little girls would grow up and, although I would remain very shy, I looked at them in a different way. I was starting to grow up.

The Bull

His name was Bull Fuller, and he played center on the basketball team. Although he was not real tall, maybe six feet, he left people lying in the lane when he went to the basket. In football, he played fullback, running out of the old Notre Dame Box; he should have been mostly a blocking back, but for some reason, when he was near the goal line, the coach found a way to get him the ball. Bull ran just like a rampaging bull. He could really hurt some people, when he ran through the line.

In 1946, we were playing a team that was two classifications above our school; it was a muddy field, and the game was very close. Late in the game, we were on about the opposing team's five-yard line; the hand-off went to Bull. He was knocked out of bounds somewhere around the two-yard line.

The out of bounds was lower than the field level, and water had collected just off the field. The whole opposing team must have landed on him. When they finally got them off of him, Bull was mad; he was screaming, "They tried to drown me!" We won the game when he scored the next play that we ran.

He was that covered in Alabama orange red clay, you couldn't tell who he was. He was some kind of big man.

The Black Mare — 1947, Sibleyville

I had ridden this black mare many times. She was a full 17 1/2 hands tall, which is very tall. She was also the fastest horse in the county, and had raced at some tracks when she was three years old! Now five, she was extremely smart. My Uncle Bill promised he would give me this horse if I would work on the farm that summer for him, which I did for 2 1/2 months.

I went back to school that September. One day, I came home from school. The black mare always met me at the lower edge of the pasture and she wasn't there.

My uncle had traded her to a man in Warrior. My dad had come home from work and had told my Uncle Bill he had better leave before I came home. I was terribly hurt that he would do this. The man who bought her bred the black mare and she had a beautiful colt.

After my uncle did this to me, it set back my faith in my fellow man. My Dad and Mom knew this had hurt me very badly. I had worked very hard all summer. The black mare had become very attached to me and she understood almost everything I said her. I could ride her anywhere without a bridle. All I had to to do was touch her on the side of her neck, and she would turn that way. If I said, "Ho, gal!" she stopped immediately. She was one smart horse. From the day I first saw her, I knew she was special. We never had a horse like her again.

I guess the thing I loved best about her was she was so fast, and her initial lunge from a standing start to full speed was awesome. Strange, as much as I loved this horse, I never gave her a name. She was always referred to to as "the black mare". She was a great horse, and to be loved, the way I loved her, was enough for her. One long whistle, and she always came running. She was the most gentle horse I've ever known.

Nell, Wild As A March Hare — 1947

The Coaldale Creek ran at the back of our house when we lived on the farm in Sibleyville. About fifty feet from our back porch was a bluff overlooking the creek. The drop below to the water was about twenty-five feet. You just didn't want to fall in it.

One day, someone had tied our horse, a sway-backed quarter horse named Nell, near the bluff. I walked by and it must have startled her. The next thing I knew, I was hurtling through the air. She had kicked me with both feet and I was falling to the creek below.

The water wasn't very deep. Just before hitting the water, I flattened my body out and did the world's biggest belly flop. It knocked all the air out of me, but worst of all was where her hooves hit me during her kick; there were two perfect hoof marks on my left hip and leg that later turned black. I know I must have lain in that water for five minutes before attempting to get up, walk down stream to a wagon ford, and then exit the creek. When I finally got back up to the house, my mom couldn't believe what had happened.

Nell was a strange horse, and about six months later, my Uncle Bill was riding her and would be thrown off her back while crossing this same creek on a wooden bridge. He landed in the water but broke his arm. Not long after this, Nell would move on to another owner. We couldn't afford the doctor bills.

The Fisherman — 1947

My dad loved to fish. He would sit in a boat all day without catching anything. He was the eternal optimist. A fish was going to bite any minute. You had to love him. He had compassion for everyone. One of his favorite places for a fishing trip was a place called Lost Lake near the Tennessee border in North Alabama. They said there was a town beneath the water in this lake. He told me it was true.

He would sit sometimes and tell me stories about the war in France in 1917. He was in the 101st Rainbow Division and fought in the Battle of the Argonne Forest. He was decorated for several battles. He was one brave man. He always made me feel that I was important in his life. He didn't hide his love for me. I remember he said to me, "You're a good son, and I'm proud of you."

One day, when I was 15 years old, I was playing with a semi-pro baseball team. I had a sprained ankle. No one could get a hit from the pitcher of the team we were playing. I told our manager I could hit him. He said to bat for this guy. I stepped in the batter's box. My dad said from behind the back stop, "You can hit him." The first pitch I swung, the ball arced deep down the left field line. I went around first and trotted to second base. My dad was hollering, "Way to go, son. Way to go." In that moment, I felt his pride and almost cried.

Warrior High School — 1948

The field was new. We finally had a very good football and baseball stadium, and the grass was starting to fill in nice and thick. We had all looked forward to this game. This was to be our year. We had a lot of experience, and some of the best players we had ever had. The national anthem was played, and we all trotted to our positions. It was time for the opening game of 1948.

I received the football on about the fifteen-yard line. I went straight up the middle for about twenty yards, cut to the left side line, and appeared in the open at about the fifty-yard stripe. About five yards further on, I was hit suddenly, by someone I never saw. I went off the field, my left shoulder hitting first in soft clay, snapping my collar bone — END OF SEASON — ONE PLAY.

The Coach

He was about six feet, four inches tall, and wore a size 13 shoe. He was slim, but was also very mobile for a person of his age, which was probably around fifty years old.

He was my football coach at Warrior High School. He was also my baseball coach and my basketball coach, and if we had had any other sport, he would have coached that as well. In the Forties and early Fifties, most schools had one coach for all sports, who also taught at least one class. His was math. He was one smart man, but he could for some reason never remember my name. He always called me Jack. I just finally started answering to whatever he called me.

I recall one time he said, "Jack, you would be a terrific running back if you could get some of the lead out of the seat of your pants." He was still there when I left to move to Gardendale in 1948.

I've often wondered where he spent his last years as a coach. He tried hard, and was really thought of highly by all who played for him. His name was Barto Hughes, and I will not forget him. I believe a lot of people who played for him feel the same way.

Odds and Ends

While living on our farm, we had this dog named Trailer. He followed my Uncle Bill, who was a horse trader, sixty miles to a town named Gadsen, arriving at a farmer's market. My uncle tied him to his wagon with a rope. That night Trailer chewed through the rope, and two days later, was back home on our farm. He was one smart dog. (This is the same uncle who sold my horse one day without my permission and kept the money. This occurred while I was at school; he left before I came home.)

In the years 1942-43-44 and during World War II, the most famous woman in America was Rosie the Riveter. In 1949, a Coke™ cost 5 cents, a movie was 10 cents, a candy bar or pack of gum was five cents. Gas was 15-17 cents a gallon. A nice car cost $650-$800. A teacher could punish you with a wooden paddle. Boys chased girls, not the other way around. Most girls wore dresses. The strangest girl's name I ever heard was Leocadia, first name only. This name derived from her grandfather's and grandmother's first names.

I attended school in Warrior, Alabama. My favorite subject was football. All the other subjects didn't seem important then. I would complete my education in the Air Force, which I joined in 1950. If I close my eyes, I can still see myself getting off the school bus, walking up the steps of the high school, then hearing Bobby Gillespie's voice, "Billy Jack, wait for me."

A Man of Great Love and Compassion

We had gone through many things together, and although my dad was a very uneducated person, he had all the traits of a very good man. He would do almost anything to help his fellowman. No one was a stranger to him. He said to me many times, "Poverty is bad, but there are many things worse." He never knew I felt inferior to other kids when I was small.

My dad loved all our family with a love so deep it hurt. He knew because of his lack of education that we would suffer for a long period of time or until we were able to earn our own living. He didn't try to hide this. That was why he wanted us all to get enough education to at least qualify for a decent job. He would sit with me many times and discuss what I needed to do just to survive in this land of ours. I guess he thought this hard way of life would never change. Two years later, his health would start to fail. He had worked in the coalmines for more than thirty-five years and now suffered from black lung disease. They gave him a small pension, and in his last years he lived a very happy life. I wasn't there when he died in 1950, sad to say. I missed out on the final two months that he lived on this earth. I had just finished basic training at Shepard AFB, Texas, and was with three thousand men opening a base in San Antonio, Texas when notified of his death.

This group of men would form the 30th Air Depot Wing and would soon proceed to England. My life had changed completely and I was about to see another world.

The Journey Starts

I had made up my mind when I was fifteen years old. I told my brothers, "Remember, I told you one day I'll be flying around, looking down at you picking cotton." Well that wasn't exactly true, but some of it was. When I reached the age of eighteen, one day I said to my mom, "I'm going to Birmingham and join the Air Force." She looked at me and smiled. "You're kidding," she said.

I waited until the next morning, caught the bus to town, went to the recruiting office, and after testing, was sworn in. I had to leave for training in three days. When I came home and told my family, they at first doubted I had enlisted. My mom was not too happy, but I finally convinced her it was best for me.

Three days later, I left Birmingham on the Hummingbird Express. We stopped in New Orleans for eight hours. Having been raised on a farm, I knew nothing about the French Quarter. By the time we left New

Orleans, I was totally confused about several things.

We arrived in San Antonio, Texas two days later. My training started that day, We slept on the ground the first nine days we were there. Then, they loaded us on to Greyhound buses; we had a string of buses at least a mile long. We were on our way to Wichita Falls, Texas, Sheppard AFB, where we received our training.

Six weeks later, I had completed my training. My flight, seventy-eight men, was sent to Kelly Air Force Base in San Antonio, Texas. The base had been closed since World War II. The weeds stood six feet tall around all the buildings. Our job was to clean up the base for the thousands who would come here in the months that followed. We were also forming a wing to be sent to England, but we didn't know that at the time. My life in the Air Force was just starting. Little did I realize what was to follow.

Korea 1950-1953
The Police Action

The battle lines surged up and down through Korea. There were a few times when it appeared we were about to lose. Several times, the weather turned into a proverbial snow and ice storm. Our troops were not equipped for these conditions. Our weapons were vintage World War II; the North Koreans and Chinese were better equipped in almost every way.

We established a foothold and turned the tide of the battle, driving the North Koreans back deep into their territory. It appeared we had now gained the upper-hand in this war, but little did anyone know that the Chinese were about to jump into the conflict.

When they came storming across the Yalu River, it was with overwhelming force. Soon, our armies started to fall back deep into South Korea. Loss of life was extremely heavy. We were driven into a pocket, almost into the sea. A brilliant plan by McArthur, a landing behind enemy lines from the sea, cut off Chinese supplies, and they were driven back into North Korea. There, an agreement was signed and the war ended. It was a terrible conflict. Many men lost their lives. We had fought and won another war for another country and, like the others, I doubt they were really thankful.

1950-1954
The Yanks Are Coming

"Over there, over there, send the word, send the word, over there/ That the Yanks are coming, the Yanks are coming..."

The band was playing, and people waved and hollered "good luck" and "God bless you!" as we walked up the gang plank and boarded the troop ship, *Maurice Rose*.

This was a few days after Christmas, 1950. We had left Kelly AFB, Texas, traveling by train to Fort Dix, New Jersey. Two days later, we boarded a bus for the ride to the Brooklyn shipyards. It was strange; we were excited but also afraid. Seven days and a lot of rough seas later, we stepped off the ship in South Hampton, England.

We now boarded a troop train for the ride to Burtonwood AFB, Warrington, England. The clicking of the train rails brought back memories for those who had come here before but not to the young airmen, like me. We arrived at Burtonwood the day before New Year's, 1950.

I went to my first dance that New Year's Eve night. I had no way of knowing that on New Year's Eve one year later, 1951, Kath and I would get engaged, or that I would love her so much it hurt. I can't say I liked the dance, except for the music. The "Boogie Woogie" was in full sway.

A few days later, the 30th Air Depot wing split into two wings. I was sent to Sealand AFB, 27 miles away. It was a much better base and besides, I was to meet a certain seventeen –year-old. Otherwise, there would not have been this story.

Sealand AFB, England
—First Date—

I came to Sealand AFB in 1951, after first being stationed at a large base outside Warrington, England named Burtonwood. Sealand was much smaller. A few months after arriving there, I would meet a seventeen-year-old girl who would steal my heart.

It all started with a blind date. I looked at this cute little lady and she said her name was Kathleen. She didn't have to say more. We didn't need much, just to hold each other and feel our hearts mesh together as one. This whole meeting was set in place by Robert Gilmore, who had asked another friend and me along, as the girl he was dating wanted to bring two other girls along with them. I did not know it at the time, but Kathleen's dad would have had a fit if he had known she was out with a Yank. We would cling to each other. never minding what anyone else thought. But I'm getting a little ahead of the story.

After meeting her this first time. we walked along a pathway that led to a small train stop, where we caught the train to Chester. It was our first date. The other two couples went to a dance, and as I wasn't much at dancing, we went to a movie instead. When we came out and went to the train station, to our surprise, the last train to Liverpool had already left. Kath was very upset, as her dad did not know she was dating an American.

When I told her we would take a taxi, she was shocked, as that was worth a week's wages in England. She was spending the night with her girl friend, Pat Duffy, at Waterloo. It was a great ride, as the cold weather made us cuddle together. When we arrived at Pat's house, Kath got out, she looked at me and said, "Will I see you again?" I said, "If the other guys have dates, I'll come again." Thank goodness there were other dates, otherwise, this story would have never been written, and you wouldn't be reading it.

Sealand AFB, England, 1951
— Hit by a Car and Survived —

This little base was split in the middle by a main highway, which would prove to be a problem for me, as you will see later in this story. I was nineteen years old and had played all sports in high school. I played football for the base team as a running back, while in baseball I pitched and played third base. I was fairly good at both sports.

After I had met Kath, and we had a date set up, I would catch the bus on the highway outside the main gate for Birkenhead, which was across the Mersey River from Liverpool. There was a large hump in the road where trains ran under the roadway, about one hundred yards from the crossing near the front gate.

I had stopped and looked in both directions, dropped my head and started across the road. Suddenly, out of the corner of my eye, I saw a reflection. I dove to the side of the road while my legs were scissored at impact. I went up in the air and saw the car go under me. The ground rushed up to meet me. At the last second, my athletic instinct took over and I relaxed, bounced once on the road, then off to the left. I was hurt, but not close to what it could have been. The driver was speeding along in a Jaguar. Kath would come see me in the hospital, and I recovered in about two weeks. Sometimes you are blessed—this was one of those times.

The River Dee — You and Me

A week after I met Kathy, we went on a picnic along the River Dee at Chester, a small town about ten miles from Sealand AFB, where I was stationed. The main street through the town led down to the river. A footbridge crossed just upstream and led to a meadow at the river's edge.

I had brought fried chicken with me from the dining hall on base and a radio that looked like a small suitcase. Radio Luxemburg was the best station available. We lay in the grass in the meadow. It was a fairly warm day, and it was great just to lie there talking about almost anything, holding hands and sharing our happiness with each other. A friend, Vince Noto, from East Illinois, and his girlfriend had come with us.

Years later, we would go by his house, on our way to Alabama from the base I was stationed at in South Dakota. He, like us, had a house full of kids, and was living a happy life.

Kathy and I would meet almost anywhere to be together. Her dad still didn't know about me. As I look back on it now, it was like a dream. I loved her and she loved me; we would find a way to marry. We just didn't know it was going to be so tough. But good things are worth waiting for, and on our wedding day, everything melted away. We had found that happiness very few would ever know.

— Yes, We Do —

The wedding car pulled up outside the entrance to the church. She stepped out, with her dad assisting with her dress. The smile on her face was beautiful. This was her day, as well as my own. In a short while we would be married in the vestry. I wasn't Catholic, so we could not be married at the altar.

The wedding started with these words, "Do you, Billy, take this lady, Kathleen, to be your lawful, wedded wife?" I remember as Father Brady spoke in his Irish brogue, I thought to myself, "I hope I understand what he's saying." We were kneeling at a small altar and I was thinking what a great moment this was in our lives. We had waited almost two years for this time to come. Then, it was over, and I held her in my arms as Mrs. Kathy Marsh.

As we were leaving the church, I asked if we could take a picture as we walked down the isle. Father Brady said, "Billy, me boy, you know it's against the rules, but if I do not see you, I cannot stop you." The pictures were taken by the photographer and turned out great. The reception was held at Kath's bridesmaid's mom's house. Mrs. Duffy did a great job. Afterwards, we all went to a pub to celebrate. A few drinks and a few laughs, then we were gone to start a special time together.

Ireland, 1953

In 1953, just a few months after we were married, we decided to go to Ireland on a late honeymoon. We flew from Liverpool to Dublin. It was a magnificent city. I remember we ate at a restaurant overlooking the main street that ran through Dublin. I had a steak. They served wine with the meal and kept filling the large goblet. Soon, I was to say the least, very tipsy.

We went on several bus tours throughout this beautiful country. We started out by going to Glendalough and then to County Cork. We rode several times in a jaunting cart. We also went to Lake Killarney, to visit the Blarney Stone. We stayed in what they call a bed-and-breakfast; it was very nice. When we stood on the side of a hill in Killarney, we could look down a valley. At the bottom stood a beautiful small castle on the edge of the lakes. It was a wonderful time of our lives. We weren't alone, though— Janet traveled with us, safely tucked away in her mommy's tummy.

Five Pounds and a Checkered Jacket

Gegs, my brother-in-law, was 15 years old the year I met Kath. That summer, he wanted to go on vacation, but could not afford the trip. I would end up loaning him five pounds plus my jacket. Jobs and money were very tight during these years. Gegs, working as a trainee electrical engineer, made less than two pounds a week or five dollars and 60 cents a week. He would enjoy the vacation, and that was what was important. He would never give me back that five pounds, but would repay me a thousand-fold since those days.

I remember the night we sat up together, while Kath was in Park House Nursing Home having our baby, Janet; I remember he was more nervous than I was. For years, we have returned to visit him and his family. Lil, his wife, is a wonderful person, and their children, Jim, Andrew and Lisa, are now grown up, married, and have given their dad and mom grandchildren. They're a very close and loving family.

I think by now you could say the five pounds has been repaid. Through Gegs' and Lily's encouragement and a slight demand for a good education, Jim and Andrew have done well — Jim as a criminal lawyer and Andrew in corporate law. Lisa continued her education and received her degree in teaching. All in all, they have done well.

If you're ever in Formby, England, stop by. You will find them there surrounded by eight beautiful grandchildren. Jim is married to Julie, who is a great wife and mommy to two lovely daughters and twin boys. Andrew married his lovely wife named Gail, and they have one son and two daughters. Lisa married a really nice guy named Ian and they have a beautiful baby girl.

Sealand AFB, England 1951-1954

I would come to this base in 1951 when we crossed the ocean on the troop ship *Maurice Rose* during seven days of rough seas. A few months after arriving, I would meet a seventeen-year-old girl, who would steal my heart.

It all happened on a blind date. I looked at this cute little lady; she said her name was Kathleen. She didn't have to say more. I loved her that instant. We didn't need much, just to hold each other and feel our heart beats mesh together as one. We would, after convincing her dad, get married. We were made for each other.

We married in an old church in a small town named Waterloo. We were so happy. It was like playing house, all we did those first few days was look at each other and smile. Although we didn't plan it this way, she would become pregnant with our first daughter, Janet. She was born at Park House

Nursing Home, Waterloo, England on December 3, 1953, and she was a beauty. Kathleen's dad loved her more than life itself.

Before we left England to return to the USA, Kathleen would become pregnant with Debbie. She was our second beautiful little girl. She would be born in Montgomery, Alabama. We were wasting no time in starting our family.

Sealand AFB, 1952 – <u>SHAZAM</u>

Our commanding officer's name was Fred B. Marvel. He had the same name as Captain Marvel in the comic books, but did not wear a cape. He was, in fact, a very gentle type of person, but, also a loner. One night, he was the officer of the day, which meant he would accompany the sergeant of the guard on inspection of all the guard posts.

Sealand was a supply base, and thievery of cigarettes and other rationed items had been occurring at night from the warehouses on base. (One guard had,in fact, been hit over the head by a thief.) That night was moonless, and the English fog had rolled in, thick and heavy. Visibility was very low. As Captain Marvel and the sergeant were approaching a guard post, a command rang out — "Halt, stand in front of your lights. Now, who goes there?" The wrong response came without thinking from the captain's mouth – "Captain Marvel." The guard's answer to this was, "Advance and be recognized, mother-blank, this is Batman!"

This really happened, and for months, jokes were played on this poor captain. Many times people would holler out "Shazam" when they saw him coming, since "Shazam" was what Captain Marvel in the comics would say, when he was transformed into his super-hero role.

Gunter AFB, Montgomery Ala., 1954-1958

I would re-enlist at Gunter AFB, for four more years, this would be a really good assignment. We loved where we were; the only exception to our happy times was when Kathleen's dad died suddenly on March 11th, 1955. The only grandchild he would ever know was Janet. It was a terrible shame he died so young. Debbie would be born on January 30th, two months prior to his death.

When we arrived in Montgomery, we moved into an old colonial home. The columns on the porch were at least twenty feet tall. Inside were three very large rooms and a kitchen. The living room must have been twenty-five feet long; large pocket doors that rolled into the walls divided the rooms. The doors and walls were about twelve feet high.

This house had a lot of room for kids to play in. The yard on both sides of the house at least eighty yards long and thirty yards wide. The first year, I used a push mower to cut two circle putting greens at the front and back of the house. It wasn't a golf course, but it allowed me to chip and putt.

Jan, and later, Debbie, would try to emulate their dad by putting the ball. Although we only lived there for three and half years, it was a great assignment. For the first two years there was only Janet and Debbie. Then Donna was born. (She looked like no one in our family. She was covered with hair.) She had long black hair, but in a few years she would start to look like her mom, Kathleen.

I had applied to retrain in jet aircraft about six weeks before Donna was born, and I was sent to Chenault AFB in Illinois after graduation. I came home and packed up and proceeded to Westover AFB in Massachusetts. This led to our first experience with snow. The weather was brutal in the winter; this would be remembered as our worst assignment, and except that our Judy was born here in 1959 at Chicopee Falls, this assignment would have been awful. We would luck out and in that year received orders for Brize Norton, England. I was promoted to staff sergeant en route to our new base. Life was much better in England. It was a great four years. Billy Jack Jr. was born in 1961: He was funny, he was pudgy. He was a beautiful boy, and the girls would spoil him rotten. So did his mom.

A few years ago while traveling through Montgomery, we went by the house we had lived in at 2215 Winona Avenue. The house was being restored. It will be beautiful when it's finished. The people who were there invited us in to take a look. The memories flooded my mind as I walked through the house, and I know it must have been the same for my wife, Kathy. When we moved into this house, it was fifty-two years ago. We have lived almost a lifetime since we left there.

Gunter AFB
Born to Lose

He was only seventeen years old, and had been in the Air Force for over a year. He had entered the service under fraud of enlistment. I still laugh today, over fifty years ago. He stole a sergeant's civilian shoes. They were brown, and although the uniform was worn with black shoes, he wore those brown shoes to his court martial and they found him innocent. How, I don't know.

He was born outside Boston, Massachusetts and his name was James Murray. We met in 1956, while serving in the same squadron in England. It was obvious he had been brought up in a tough area, but even I wasn't ready for what would happen four years later.

Kilby Prison was across the road and less than half a mile from Gunter AFB's main entrance. We had a very good fast-pitch softball team on base. Kilby Prison challenged us to play them. We were to find out that they were more than good, as their pitcher threw a double-header shutout against us.

I was running around in the outfield, catching and returning balls during batting practice, when I collided with a prisoner. I was on my hands and knees and so was he. He looked at me, and then we both spoke. "You're Bill," he said. All I could say was, "James Murray." I found out during a short conversation they allowed us, he had come down to Mobile, Alabama to work. In the process of breaking into a warehouse one night, a guard caught him, and he killed the guard. I really felt bad for him, but after I thought about it, I should have not been surprised.

Montgomery, Alabama
Martin Luther King, Jr. — 1954

I had returned from England with my wife Kathleen and our baby daughter, Janet. When I had gone to Lake Charles, Louisiana and returned after 17 days, I would re-enlist in the Air Force at Maxwell AFB in Alabama, where I would be stationed for a few years. We spent many happy moments during this assignment. During our stay in Montgomery, Debbie and Donna were born. It seemed our family would increase each year.

The first time I heard his name, it really didn't mean anything to me, for I was sure he was no more or less than the black leaders that I had seen before. They promised the Negroes their freedom. How wrong I was, for he would become the very symbol that would lead his people out of the dark ages and into a new life and pride in their heritage.

He preached non-violence and this tactic was the very thing that the bigots of the United States could not attack. For how could anyone fight against a man that said, "let my people be free." I remember a black airman that worked with me, who said, "He is not a normal, run-of-the-mill man, for he is sure that in the near future we shall overcome this hatred and prejudice that have been on my people's shoulders for many years."

In Montgomery, Alabama, he launched his first campaign for freedom. He would at first attack the segregated bussing system by refusing to ride the buses. This was at first laughed at, but as the months dragged on and they continued to walk rather than ride segregated buses, it became obvious that the bus company would go broke. So, after nine months, the bus company agreed to desegregate the bussing system. He had won his first victory for his people.

No one but he knew the dangers and suffering he went through during this time. He was thrown in jail and his home was bombed. Even the church where he preached was blown up. I am sure that as I look back now I had no sympathy for this man, but I soon started to respect him. In the next few years, I followed his activities with great interest.

Although I know now I was as prejudiced as anyone, and I am sure that some of my childhood prejudices are still with me today, I feel that he at least has taught me to respect the black man as my equal; through his teachings, the black race has moved forward in our society. The prejudices that have existed in our great country are now slowly dissipating.

Like he said in one of his last speeches, he had been to the mountaintop. I feel he didn't go there alone, for he took his entire race with him, and I am sure that there were a few million whites that stood and applauded him. In Memphis, he was to meet his final fate; his work now almost done, he died at the hand of an assassin. History will record that he was a great man, not just for the black man, but also for all humanity. And now as I write this book, I know that I speak for millions of the white race of people: it was an honor to have been there as he moved forward, always forward.

How's That Possible?

We had left Alabama and were now on the New Jersey Turnpike, which led to the George Washington Bridge that crossed over into the Bronx, New York. Kath's girlfriend, who was also her bridesmaid in England in

1953, had come to New York a year or so after we returned to the USA, in 1954. Now married to a police officer, their home was here in the Bronx. I had no idea where they lived.

After exiting the bridge, I passed a service station. I turned right into a street after a block or so. I used someone's driveway to turn around, and returned to the service station, where I checked the directory for Pat and her husband's phone number.

He answered the phone, and said he knew where we were. I still can't believe we had driven twelve hundred miles, turned around in a driveway in New York, and it was the house we were going to visit but had no idea where it was.

The odds of this happening would be millions to one.

The Colored Water Incident

We had returned from England and were stationed at Gunter AFB in Montgomery, Alabama. Debbie and Donna, our second and third daughters, would be born here.

In 1955, Kathy's dad died suddenly, leaving her younger brother Jerry and sister Veronica (Roni) on their own. Jerry was about to receive his draft call-up into the Royal Air Force, and this would leave Roni alone at home. As she was only seventeen years old, it was decided that she would come to Montgomery and live with us.

This worked out well for both her and Kath, as Roni was very happy living with us; she loved our three daughters (Jan, Debi and Donna) very much, and was a great help to Kath in looking after them. Roni soon found a job at Kressge's Five and Dime, and spent most of her paychecks on her nieces.

During this period, segregation was a very big issue in Montgomery; the city was in turmoil, as the black people boycotted busses and stores. This led to what we came to call "the colored water incident". Roni had only been in the States a few weeks when she and Kathy went shopping. As they approached a water fountain in a department store, she saw the signs for "White" and "Colored" on the water coolers. Roni tried both faucets, as she was curious as to what color water would be dispensed by each faucet. You can imagine the laugh that ensued after that!

In 1958, we were reassigned to Westover AFB, Massachusetts. Roni had made friends with some wonderful people, and she decided to stay in Montgomery, but in 1959, she changed her mind, and moved up to Massachusetts to live with us. Not long after this, we received orders reassigning us to England.

Roni decided to return to Alabama and attend a Bible college to become a teacher. It was during this time frame that she met James, the man who would become her husband. They had two sons who gave them three grandchildren: Victoria and Michael, from Steven, the oldest son; and Olivia Kate, from Daniel and his cutie-pie wife Solita.

When we returned to the States in 1963, we were stationed at Ellsworth AFB, near Rapid City, South Dakota. Each year we would travel down to Alabama, and our first stop was Decatur, to visit Roni and James. They were always waiting for our arrival. By now, we had five children, and needless to say, Roni was waiting to spoil all of them! Now, fifty years later, we still make trips to Alabama, and James and Roni come visit us in Florida; we try to spoil their grandchildren, when we are around them.

Our lives have come full circle, and it all began in England in 1951, when I met Kath on a blind date. Life really is strange—without that date, so long ago now, all these things would never have happened.

POST SCRIPT: As this story is being finished, Solita and Daniel are expecting their second child: more joy is on the way!

The Year at Westover —Judy Born

In 1958, I was assigned to Westover AFB in Chicopee Falls, Massachusetts. This was my first taste of really cold weather. Judy, our fourth daughter, would be born here and in about thirteen months we would ship out to England—but, that was still thirteen months away. In the meantime, we were terribly short of money.

We were paid once a month, and after rent and a car payment, we were left with less than $150.00 for food and clothes, gas for the car and any other expenses. One time, we ran completely out of food and the lady who rented our apartment to us found out through Janet, who was playing outside. She took the kids inside and fed them. It was payday, and when I got home late that day, we went to the store and came home and fixed supper. The kids loved hamburgers, and that's what we had.

It was a tough thirteen months, and when we left there for England, we really celebrated. I never wanted to go back to Massachusetts again. My only regret was I never wrote back to tell the old French Canadian couple who rented us the apartment and were so kind to my children, how much Kath and I appreciated what they did for us.

One good thing did happen while at Westover. In 1959, Judy the trooper was born. This little gal would prove to be the Marsh team cheerleader, and today carries the spirit of the Marsh clan in her mind and heart, for she is truly of the Marsh bloodline. Aggressiveness with a touch of compassion, and feeling for all around her, will carry her wherever she wants to go. Not long after she was born, we were on our way to England. We were all happy, and my Kathleen was going home.

James Stewart — "Cowbell 57"

I had only been at Westover AFB six months. One day while pre-flighting the B-52 I was assigned, our commander came by, and said, "Your plane has been chosen for a movie starring James Stewart. He will be coming by shortly." Sure enough, Stewart came riding up in a car a short time later. He stepped out, stood looking at the plane, and then walked over. He was dressed in an overcoat and hat. He appeared to be a little slump-shouldered. He asked if I objected to appearing in a movie he was about to make. I said, "No." He said it wouldn't be a speaking part.

A few hours later, he drove up in a staff car, got out with five crew members, walked over and asked for the aircraft forms and stood there studying them. Then he said, "Good job." I said, "Thank you." All at once, I realized I had just spoken in this movie after all.

The next day, when they came back, I asked, "What's the name of the movie?" "*Cow Bell 57*," they said. I later learned that that was the aircraft call sign. I didn't have much contact with him after this, but all signs pointed to him being a really nice man. I never saw the movie, but a few years later one of my nephews saw it one night on TV. This was my one and only time as a movie star.

In 1963, Rock Hudson and a movie company came to Ellsworth AFB to make a movie called *The Strategic Air Command*. It was a really big production. This was during the years when almost everyone was a true patriot. On the day they were to start filming, it started to snow. It was early spring, and this time of the year was noted for blizzards. As they tried to continue filming, the storm became worse; after three days, they finally gave up, stating no one could operate in this kind of weather. They left, and went to March AFB in California to complete the movie. I never appeared in this movie, but I felt we were connected, if only in a small way.

3-Minute Warning

During my stay at Brize Norton (1959-1963), I would serve as a flight chief on reflex alert B-47 bombers on 24-hour-a-day nuclear alert. This was Europe's first line of defense. It was always felt we might not get all the bombers airborne before we were hit by Russian missiles, not a comforting thought.

We also had a spy outfit from Kansas that had one aircraft, an R-B 47. We didn't know exactly what he was doing, but one day when he didn't return from his flight, things became hectic. Later we were told he was shot down over the Bering Straits by Russian MiG fighters. The name of this spy group was OL-1. It was said they fired back when attacked by the MiG fighters, and may have shot one down. Russia never admitted they shot down one of our planes.

It really didn't matter if they admitted that they had shot down the RB-47. An RC 135 flying a hundred miles further out over the Bering Straits monitored the radio conversation where the MiGs moved in for the kill. No radio transmission was heard from the RB-47, but that was not unusual. These missions were flown in total radio silence. None of the aircraft or crew was ever recovered. It had gone down in a very remote region of the arctic circle.

A few days later, another RB-47 arrived at Brize Norton and the flights would continue. Their mission was to probe the coastline of Russian territory. As soon as a radar locked on to the RB-47, they would break away and denote the exact location of the radar site. Their whole purpose was to find the gaps in Russia's radar system in case of war.

So Very Close — 1962

Flash. "This message is in two parts — scramble, scramble, scramble. Part two kilo tango" — "Charlie break-break" hurry – hurry – launch – climb to ten thousand – positive control at point – razor – we had scrambled at 02:00 hours. This was not a drill. The landing lights blinked three times on the ten B-47 bombers; some did not wait for the chocks to be removed, but instead went to full power and jumped the chocks. It was, to say at the least, a very scary moment.

The planes flowed to the end of the runway. We were all waiting for them to stop. My radio crackled in my vehicle. "What's going on out there maintenance one?" "I can't answer that. I'll call you by phone."

Then three aircraft were on the runway. Engines went to full power. ATO bottles fired; as the fourth plane pulled on the runway, he suddenly pulled back his throttles. The launch had stopped. We had three planes airborne. They would return. There was no war.

Weeks after this, we were to find out what happened. There had been an explosion on the B-mews early warning system in Alaska. NORAD had notified the Strategic Air Command that the probability of an attack on the USA was high. SAC then started to launch the bombers that would be hit first. There were a lot of happy faces at breakfast that morning.

England, 1961 —
7 Follyview Crescent, Farrington

The house was a beautiful cottage. We had moved here from Enysham, a house called the Studio. This cottage was perfect for our family. In the back was a garden with a small lawn, which was perfect for the kids to play on. There was a nice little village at the bottom of the hill, and a school was nearby for the kids. Our neighbors were nice people.

Kath's brothers would show up on surprise visits — we never knew when they were coming. Jim and Gegs loved the kids, and gave the kids nicknames. Some were called "pee-pee pants" some were "dukie legs". The kids really loved them.

When I came home one day, Billy had fallen off the bunk beds and injured himself. When I touched his shoulder, I knew at once that the collar bone was broken. He soon got over it, though, and was back doing all his funny things.

In the summer, the kids would swim in a stream near the town. To say our lives were exciting with all the kids doesn't really cover what it was like. Many times, we picnicked along the Thames River. The kids, along with other children, played and swam. It was a beautiful place to live. An older couple lived next door. They appeared to liked us, or at least they appeared to, while we were living there.

One day, Donna got a bottle of diet pills belonging to her mom or one of the neighbors. She took the whole bottle. We had to rush her to the hospital, but on the way, she threw up the pills. She was really sick to her stomach, but otherwise OK. I'm sure she didn't gain any weight for the next year or so.

1962
Perfection—Maybe Just Too Good??

In 1962, I had been chosen to attend NCO Leadership School. We would be graded over a one-month period at this school on the subjects of drill and ceremony, speech, education, and leadership. The first speech was tough — a one-minute speech about yourself, with penalties for timing and a five-minute speech followed by drill, then leadership presentation, and education. The commandant's award would be given to the over-all winner.

I won the drill award, then the speech award, and was elected class spokesman. The award contest for leadership was a split between another man and me, but I had fewer inspection demerits. He won the education award on the night of graduation. Most were shocked when this guy won the commandant's award. He looked across the stage at me; I could read in his eyes that he was sorry he received the award. It was too late — politics had won again.

The Grand National

One of the things celebrated each year in England is the Grand National Horse Race: forty horses, 4 ½ miles plus five hundred yards, thirty giant fences. To finish the race is quite a feat; to win it is tremendous. And if you have a small wager on it and you win, you celebrate. Almost everybody has a bet with the local bookmaker.

I put a pound on four horses and smiled when the kids picked out their horses, using the name as the best way. Debbie picked Ayala at 100-1; Jan had Hawaii's Song at 20-1. I don't know if the other kids had a bet.

Anyway, my horses all fell. Janet's was leading a fence from home, but ended up third. She won five shillings. Debbie's horse won at 100-1 and paid five pounds, which was 14 dollars for 14 cents' bet. They were really thrilled. I was happy for them, but not too happy for myself. That's why I always thought they should name it "The Grand Disaster".

Brize Norton, England
The Cherokee Indian, 1960-1963

They said his temper had a very short fuse, and they were right. I thought I saw his hands move, but I wasn't sure. The one thing I did know was that a staff sergeant was lying on the ground, and Carl was standing over him and saying, "You want to repeat that statement again?" This was not normal Air Force discipline, but it was one of this Indian's ways of getting your attention. Carl would, a year later, try this same tactic on me, but I taught him a lesson. I grabbed a B-4 stand jack handle and told him, "You put a hand on me, and I'll beat you to death." He knew I meant it, and walked away.

He could have been a first-rate supervisor, except for one fault — he had to have someone to ride. Once he realized you were the one, he made your life miserable. I really felt sorry for one particular flight chief, because Carl would insult him in front of his men. I begged this guy to challenge Carl, but he was afraid of him.

Carl was married to a real Cherokee princess. She was beautiful, and just the opposite of him, but, he never challenged her. When he left Brize Norton and returned to the States, the man who replaced him was just the opposite of him. Everyone took a deep breath — life was now normal.

Follow Me

Darkness was falling over this base situated on a plateau nine miles east of Rapid City, South Dakota. I had arrived here back in 1963, and it was now nearly 1970. We had a 12,000-foot runway plus two 500-foot overruns, one on each end of the runway. I was sitting in a metro step van that was used as a "follow me" vehicle. The taxiway that ran the full length of the runway was slightly uphill, running to the northwest.

We had had a small snowfall that afternoon. We had seen far worse hundreds of times in the last ten years, but still it made things a little slippery. Little did we know, though, that coming down this slight grade from the northwest, it was more than a little slippery.

About two thousand feet up the taxiway, where the grade was steepest, the runway surface was pure black ice. To make things worse, there was a wind of about twenty-five knots at the back of a B-52 that had just landed. If the pilot had retracted his flaps and lowered the air brakes on top of the wings, the wind would have affected the aircraft far less. But he didn't, and now we were about to have a disaster on our hands.

Parked lengthwise near the middle of the taxiway was a KC-135 tanker. If the B-52 didn't stop, it was going to plow into this aircraft fully loaded with fuel. All at once, the B-52 entrance hatch opened, and I saw crew- members falling out on the ground and then rolling out of the way of the gears and tires. The B-52 was now out of control. As it rolled along, ground crew members were throwing four-foot chocks under the wheels, which were then spit out with tremendous speed.

It was now heading directly at the tanker and gaining speed. Only a miracle could avert this awful accident. I had just told our control to have the fire department ram the aircraft, but unknown to us, the miracle we needed was found in the shape of a 150-pound fire extinguisher known as the Big Bertha. Regulations required each parked plane to have one of these fire-bottles (which were mounted on two-wheeled dollies) nearby; this one was a short distance from the B-52's side of the tanker. As the aircraft neared the Big Bertha, the extinguisher went between the two tires on the left forward landing gear, scrubbing against them. It stopped the plane less than ten feet from the tanker.

Today, more than thirty-five years later, I still can't believe that fire bottle stopped that B-52. When the plane finally came to a full stop, the gunner in the tail jettisoned his turret and came sliding down a rope. Boy, what a red face he had.

Assignment to Ellsworth AFB, South Dakota

In 1963, we returned to the USA. We had been assigned to a base in South Dakota named Ellsworth. Little did I realize we would be stationed here until 1974, leave for one year, and return for one more year before I retired. The children would all attend Douglas High School and all four girls would graduate there. For years we camped out in the Black Hills on Paktola and Sheridan Lakes. The lakes were full of rainbow trout and we enjoyed them barbequed. Billy and I just loved to catch them.

When winter came, we would come to Sheridan Lake, set up an ice skating racetrack for the kids, start a fire out on the ice, and roast hotdogs and marshmallows. It was a really good life. One year I left the hose running all night to flood a low spot in the back yard for a skating rink. It worked so well, it flooded across a main road and put a sheet of ice on it. Another year, all the kids wanted to take cookies and candy to all the guards who were guarding the flight line and alert force. It was Christmas Eve, and the young men guarding the planes loved it. I had a Santa suit on, and as we approached the alert force gate, the guard didn't know what to do. He called his supervisor for help. They finally let us in and escorted us from guard to guard. It was a great night.

Another time, it was decided to produce a play for all the children on Ellsworth AFB. That year the British girls, along with Frank Herner, myself and several other people, put on the play *Cinderella*. It was a great success. Kath and one other lady were dressed as the ugly sisters and had the kids in the audience really excited. The next year, we produced *Dick Whittington*, when Kath got to play the lead role, Dick Whittington.

Judy decided to go out for the track team one year, and as always, we supported anything they did. She wasn't the best, but she tried hard. Donna competed in gymnastics. She did well. Judy also tried gymnastics, but she wasn't sold on their coach. As Billy grew, he would want to play football, and became good on defense and as a wide receiver.

One year, in a kite-flying contest, Billy and I made a huge kite, and as I had an unlimited supply of 500-pound test nylon cord. We launched our kite that morning on the hill leading out of Rapid City to the west of town. After the kite climbed about 2000 feet upward, it started to travel east over the city. We tried to reel it in but it was impossible. When the cord finally broke, it came down across town, approximately four miles away. We had won the contest and the new bike that came as the prize, but couldn't prove it — our cord could not be rewound and measured, so we actually lost.

You're Not the Boss of Me

Judy was not more than six or seven years old. She was a spitfire. She, more than any of my children, displayed her Indian heritage. Cross her at the wrong time or place, and instant war would erupt. She had this love for her sisters and her brother and was ready to fight to defend them no matter who you were. I remember well the close brother-and-sister bond that existed between her and Billy. I still laugh today about all her antics. She was one tough kid.

One day, I was laying down the law with all my kids. "You won't do this and you won't do that," I exclaimed. "I'm the boss in this household. No one else." Not a word was uttered by Janet, Debbie, Donna or Billy, but then, lo and behold, out of Judy's mouth came this statement, "You're not the boss of me." I exploded. Everything I had just said, had been destroyed by her with just a few words. I can still see her — just a little girl, standing with her hand on her hips and this defiant look on her face. I'm sure I must have smiled inside.

Winston

In 1943, if you had asked who represented the staunchest stand against Germany and Japan, the answer would have been Winston Churchill, while he was in power as the prime minister of England. When he died in January 1965, his body was carried by train to a place called Woodstock, to be returned to Blenheim Palace, where he was born. He then was taken to a small village down the road, named Bladen, and on an embankment overlooking this small village, he was laid to rest — a simple little graveyard with a very small chapel in the center and a gravel path passing by at his feet.

I had flown from Ellsworth AFB in South Dakota, and landed at RAF Upper Heyford. Jim, my wife Kath's brother, had driven down from Liverpool to be with me that day. It was he who had driven me over to Woodstock, then to the gravesite, and now, as I stood looking at his grave, it hit me. Here lies one of the greatest men of our time. No splendor, no great grave marker, no headstone, just green grass that had started to sink slightly. He was buried in a coffin, nothing else. They were waiting until the grave sunk, prior to putting a marble or granite cover over the grave.

A caretaker was working nearby. I asked if they would care if I took a small piece of sod from his grave. "I don't think so, Yank," was his answer. I borrowed a knife he was using, cut out a 4-inch square piece of sod, placed it in a bag and thanked him. I looked at the grave again and said goodbye.

We left the next day, and flew back to Ellsworth AFB, South Dakota on the B-52 we had flown over. I took the piece of sod, and planted it among the Kentucky blue grass that made up the lawn at 9893-A Pringle Avenue at Ellsworth AFB, South Dakota. Within a week, you couldn't tell where it was planted, but I know it's there — so does my Kath and our children. That was more than forty years ago; and for those of us who admired him, we won't ever forget who he was, and what he stood for.

This Is a Test – 1964

The claxon blared out its loud pulsing sound. Flight crews and ground crews ran out of the chutes from underground to the surface outside, then to the ten B-52s sitting in a Christmas tree configuration. Black powder smoke filled the air as cartridge engine starters fired, and engines started. Then, over the intercom from the cockpit, came this word "chocks out," clear the aircraft. We were going to launch.

As I ran to the wing tip, I never knew if this was a real launch or not. Each plane leaped out of its parking spot, then two hundred yards later, was on the runway with full power on all eight engines. The first one to the runway rolled about two thousand feet. Then, the throttles came back, and he coasted to the runway center taxiway, and turned off. Each other aircraft did the same. Within twenty minutes, they were parked back on the alert pad to await what would come next time.

This Strategic Air Command alert condition had been in operation for more than twenty years; each plane carried four nuclear weapons, each capable of destroying any major city. Under the wings of each plane we had two hound-dog missiles, each with a nuclear weapon powerful enough to destroy a four-square-mile area. If we were attacked, retaliation would be swift. This was our job.

When we returned to the alert building, we found we were in a full operational inspection by S.A.C. Headquarters and we would fly training sortie bomb runs to demonstrate proficiency. The only thing different about this test was that they had asked the wing commander what would he do if they asked him to launch all the B-52s at night with a 15-second interval, which would mean as many as four planes would be on the runway at once, and if one aborted his takeoff, those following him could not stop to avoid running over each other. His answer was to them, blow the horn and find out. That night, about eight o'clock, the horn blew, and the alert scramble was on. As they launched, it was awesome. The sky looked like a Christmas tree with all the lights blinking from the planes. This was the first and only test of this kind ever attempted, to this day.

1964-1980
Ellsworth, 1964 — Buffy, The Shetland Sheepdog

When I picked her up, she was a little ball of fluff, black and white, with the white markings on her feet, chest, tip of her tail and stomach. She would turn out to be extremely smart. But on this night, she was a tiny puppy with all the love a little puppy dog could show to her master. I placed her inside my shirt, and she lay there, with only her head sticking out between buttons.

I should have known she would be special to our family. The kids loved her, and she would play with them all. They wanted her to sleep in their beds, but I wouldn't allow this, or so I thought. I was never sure if they snuck her up to bed with them at night.

Anyway, in six months, the house was hers, and in the winters she loved to play in the snow banks outside. We still had her when I retired from the Air Force and moved to Orange Park, Florida. The kids would grow up, get married or move out.

When she was fifteen years old, she would start to go blind and her kidneys would start to fail. She would walk into a corner of the porch or house and would become frightened. That was when I knew her life was at end. We buried her in the yard and planted a rose over her grave. With all her love, she deserved no less.

Ellsworth AFB, South Dakota
1963-1974 through 1976

These were the years of nuclear-alert, airborne chrome-dome missions flown around the clock, while half of S.A.C.'s B-52 fleet were on alert, with aircrews and ground crews in underground quarters. We were always ready to launch a nuclear strike against any enemy, but our motto was, "peace is our profession".

Then one day, in a far-off distant land called "Vietnam," someone fired the "first shot." Seven years later, 58,000 American men were dead and 300,000 were wounded. In between these years, the United States armed forces were totally consumed by this war.

In early 1965, all B-52D model bombers were cycled through Boeing's aircraft plant. We didn't know at the time, but the bomb-bays of these B52s were being enlarged, also. This revised plane was receiving a camouflage-and-black paint job when the first of them arrived back at Ellsworth. We were shocked at what it looked like. It was a complete change from silver and white.

We now knew we were about to enter the war in Vietnam. The air power used in this war was staggering: Over two hundred B-52 bombers were committed to this war, their bomb loads of 60,000 pounds each were awesome, and if used properly, could have ended the war in six months or less. But someone chose a different route.

A Beer-Friendship and a Fight

We had gone to this bar for a beer and maybe to play some pool. I had no idea we would end up in a fight. Jim Thomas and a kid named Murphy were with me. As we entered the bar, I noticed an Air Force tech sergeant with whom I'd had an argument on the flight line. He had his aircraft recovery team with him, about nine younger men.

As we played pool, Murphy said to me, "Those guys keep saying smart remarks. Are they talking to you or us?" I told Murphy I had had a problem with them a few days earlier, when they recovered my aircraft. I knew how Murphy was quick to get mad, and I tried to downplay what they were saying. But they were now getting really bold with their insults.

That's when Murphy, Jim and I turned and walked over to where they were sitting. I grabbed this tech sergeant by the shirt, pulled him up out of his seat, and slapped him backhand across the face. As I did, Murphy punched one of the most vocal of the other guys between his running lights, and was reaching for another. Meanwhile, Jim had given this big kid a karate chop and thrown him into a corner. They were all now hollering, "We are sorry, we were only joking." They all left.

A few minutes later, Charley Dick, a friend, walked into the bar. He said, "Who were those guys in the parking lot? One of them said Bill Marsh was a jerk. I told him I was your friend, and then I had to hit him for telling a lie about you."

I replied, "Have a beer, Charley, I'll drink to that."

Guam, 1966

In 1966, I would fly my first combat mission over Vietnam. As we approached the end of the runway, my heart was really thumping. A short runway and a very heavy plane make you nervous. As we pulled onto the runway, I looked straight ahead. We could see for a mile and a half down the centerline. The throttles moved forward, and we started to roll.

Down below, the navigator called, "70 knots now," and in about twenty-five seconds he said, "Coming up on unstick, ready, ready now," and I watched the aircraft commander, Herb Jordan, slightly pull back on the control column. Then he said, "Gears up," and lights flashed on, then all indicators showed up.

Fifteen seconds later, Herb Jordan said, "Start the flaps." When they were full up, we now started to accelerate: 220, 230, 250, 300 knots. Finally, we started to climb. Eight minutes later, we had reached 31,000 feet, leveled off and were soon cruising at 500 knots.

As we approached the Philippines three hours later, we could look down upon the islands that General McArthur liberated during the last days of World War II. Shortly after this, we would contact our tankers out of Kadena AFB, Okinawa, mid-air refuel, then proceed to Vietnam. We were to bomb the delta region; we could see Saigon as we neared our target. After bombs away, we banked, sharply climbed several thousand feet, and then headed for Guam. The flying and combat pay was good for the month, and I could take a deep breath and smile again.

The Trawler — 1966

For months, we had known they were there. It amazed me that we did nothing about their constant observation of our operations. Each time we launched our B-52s, we knew they would notify Hanoi, who, in turn, would contact the Vietcong in South Vietnam, who would now know our arrival time. After the war had stopped, the Vietcong revealed that the B-52 strikes were what they feared most during the Vietnam conflict.

We had been warned numerous times to take no action against the Russian trawler. That was why I was so surprised when, returning from a mission, we had received permission to fly a low-level ACR terrain avoidance run on the hill that descended down to Taragai Beach. We started our run from about five miles out. We were down to two hundred fifty feet, air speed just under 400 knots. All of a sudden, there was the trawler about a mile away, but in line with our run to Taragai Beach. As we passed over the pilot pulled the nose of the B-52 sharply upward. The gunner in the tail of the aircraft reported that the trawler almost capsized. The wing commander was not happy when he addressed the crew later; but in his eyes, we could see a slight smile.

One Mission Over Vietnam, 1967

Sunday morning at 06:00 hours, high in the clouds approaching Vietnam, I sat waiting, along with a crew aboard B-52 55-113. We had come here this Easter morning to awaken Charlie. The mission had started earlier, back on Guam. I had reported to work before midnight, pre-flighted my aircraft and as I was to ride along on this mission, it would get special treatment from my ground crew and me.

The flight crew arrived, and after their pre-flight, we started engines and taxied out. We were to fly in the second cell. As red cell pulled onto the runway, we prepared for take-off.

After the first cell was airborne, then it was our turn to go. As the engines went to full power and we started to roll, the runway would flash by, and 450,000 pounds of aircraft, fuel and bombs would become airborne.

After three hours, we were passing near the Philippines. Descending to 26,000 feet, we met our refueling tankers out of Kadena A.F.B., Okinowa. After mid-air refueling, we climbed to 29,000 feet. Our target was now two hours away. Approaching the coast of

Indochina, we turned south until we were off the coast of Vietnam. Below us, sitting off shore, was the hospital ship, *Hope*. A small river could be seen off to our right wing. We were at 29,000 feet and now starting to climb to 35,000 feet. In a few minutes, we were over Vietnam. Below us was only jungle, but we knew Charlie was there. I remember, as we neared the target and I felt the bomb doors open and heard the Radar say, "Stand by for release," thinking to myself, "My God, what an Easter present for anyone."

In the belly of our plane hung 108 five-hundred-pound bombs, and under the wings hung another 24 bombs. The big bomber shook as we started to release them.

Below us, the earth would explode, and Charlie would curl in a ball with his knees in his chest, to try and stop his intestines from exploding from the shock and roar all around him.

We waited fifteen seconds and then started a left turn, and climbed to 43,000 feet. Six hours later, we were back on Guam.

The crew would report any secondary explosions, and I would write my Kathleen that the flying and combat pay was O.K. for the month. Back in Vietnam, Charlie would by now have gathered his senses and prepared to fight again. I am sure that he was afraid, but he believed in what he was fighting for, and would continue to defy the might of the United States for another five years.

Time to Fly — Guam 1969

Time 18:00 hours, ARC light, launch fifteen B-52s. I was to fly on my friend's aircraft 56-604, also known as Blue Three. Engine start, 17:25 hours. (Command post name, Charlie)

"Charlie this is Blue Three, we have radar problems." "604 Blue Three. Blue one and two will launch on time. You will then have six minutes to launch." (Thirty minutes later) "Blue cell engine start time. 604 Blue Three, four minutes to max launch time. "Charlie 604, understand?" "Four minutes, Blue Three— are you ready to roll?" "Negative. Our BNS system is inoperative." "604 Blue Three, this is Charlie, be aware Sergeant Marsh aboard your aircraft. Must fly on one of the aircraft launching. "604 Charlie, taxi to Hammerhead. We will take Marsh off and put him on aircraft 671 Brown Three." "Charlie this is 604, we are approaching Hammerhead. BNS is now OK. I repeat, OK." "604 Blue Three, This is Charlie, launch now." "Roger. 604 rolling."

What was this all about? I had to be on board a plane that was to land at U-Tapao, Thailand returning from a bombing mission over Vietnam. I was to replace the aircraft maintenance supervisor for two weeks while he went to the States on emergency leave.

B-52s Over Laos

I noticed at the crew briefing, things were being explained a little more precisely. As we prepared to leave the briefing room, they handed us different handguns. These were automatics; also, we received four clips of ammo, plus three grenades with an extra safety pin that locked the regular pin in place. I started to wonder where we were going. The flight seemed normal until we reached altitude.

Then, they opened the flight orders. It still didn't seem too bad, as we were to bomb some bridges in Laos. Then, all of a sudden, I said, "Hey — Laos, that's not Vietnam!" The radar navigator said, "That's right, Billy." They said we would see a lot of fireworks before we reached our target. Three hours later, we were over Vietnam, then, suddenly veered slightly east.

About ten minutes later, the pilot pointed out the left window. The sky was lit up with huge searchlights. Then, suddenly, explosions by the thousands could be seen below us. The electronics warfare officer said, "SAM, SAM, SAM" over the interphone. Then, "Positive Lock," the pilot said, "stand by for evasive maneuver." Over UHF radio we heard, "Blue Cell, break left, decrease speed fifty knots." Just at that moment the radar said, "Targets in twenty seconds,":

followed by, "level the wings, open the bomb doors."

I said to myself, "There's a SAM missile tracking us, and all this guy is worried about is getting the bombs on target?" Then I heard the best news of all. The ECM operator said, "Missile guidance is jammed. Missile deflected 30 degrees." As he said this, the radar said, "Bombs away, one hundred and eight bombs jettisoned." All at once, the big bomber rose slightly in the air and shook. The pilot said, "Good job, guys. Stand by for thirty-degree left turn."

After this, we were out of Laos in a few minutes. Only then did I realize my flight suit was soaking wet with sweat. I put a flight lunch in the little oven, had a cup of coffee and settled back for the six-hour flight back to Guam.

1967
The Senator and Phony Money

In 1967, a distinguished senator came to visit us in Guam. He was the chairman of the Armed Forces Sub-Committee and was always treated with great care by the military. I received a radio call from the command post saying he was on the way out to the ramp and would be at South Ramp Spot 13. I then was told to meet him there, to show him around a B52 bomber. I always looked sharp in my white supervisor's uniform decorated with several bomb competition patches and other SAC emblems.

The staff car approached, I met them, and saluted. He stepped out and introduced himself. I had seen him before on TV; he always displayed an arrogant attitude. He followed me around the outside of the airplane and then wanted to go inside. I opened the hatch. He climbed up inside, and an officer followed him. I started the power unit and applied power to the aircraft. I had turned all the instrument lights up full.

He was visibly impressed. He started asking questions. The officer with him said, "I'll let the expert here answer your questions." After ten minutes or so, we exited the cockpit. He then asked a strange question, "I've been told we are dropping counterfeit money on North Vietnam." He answered his own question by saying, "That's not ethical; we wouldn'l do that." I asked him to wait for my answer.

I walked over to some boxes in the revetment, reached inside, and pulled out a small stack of Vietnamese dong bills, placed it in his hand, and proclaimed, "No, we would never do that." He was shocked. On the box, it said "product of Fordyce, Arkansas", which was his home state. They had sent him out to the plane that flew all the money-drop missions. He said thanks and goodbye, and then drove away. I could have told him (but

I didn't) that each time this plane flew a mission, Hanoi would come under attack by at least 15 planes, and that several specially-fitted C-130 aircraft loaded with jamming equipment would fly to the outer boundaries of the city and jam anything that was turned on, especially their surface to air missiles. One thing I will say about this senator, he was one tough guy, and really went to bat for people in the military. I guess you could say we owed him a lot.

Return From Guam

His name was Edgar Harris. He was the wing commander, and a real nice guy. When we returned from Guam one year, he had received some great reports as to our actions in support of ARC light. In fact, the commander in Guam said that if we had not been there, they would have failed to meet their combat requirements.

Edgar felt really good about us when we returned. He wanted us to know this, so we were all brought into a briefing room a few days after our return. He read each man's name out, and then proceeded to tell what his job was and what he had accomplished. When he came to me, he just smiled. I could tell his personal friendship with me gave him real satisfaction. He read, "For outstanding performance in all phases of aircraft maintenance." He then winked at me, shook my hand, and then turned to all the men, "You men have really made us proud. Dismissed."

As I left, the wing sergeant major stopped me as I neared my car. "Billy", he said, "Col. Harris would like a few words with you. He said wait here at your car." About five minutes later, Col. Harris drove up in his staff car. He said, " I would like to talk to you if you have a few minutes," and he motioned for me to get into his car. We rode toward his office.

The Colonel asked me a question, "Tell me, were these other wings who had come to replace us when we last rotated home really bad?" I replied, "Colonel, you asked and this is the truth. They are the worst of the worst. For some reason, they have never faced adversity. Everything they do is slow and methodical. They would get so behind, there was no catching up. They just didn't understand you can't do everything by the book. This is war, plain and simple. You do what you must to meet mission requirements." He looked at me and said, "Thanks. I know I can always depend on you."

The President

The President of the United States, Gerald Ford, stopped off at our base, Ellsworth AFB, during his re-election campaign. He had left Denver that morning and would refuel before proceeding to Washington. He had told his people on board the aircraft he wanted to meet some of the service people. When he arrived, I was selected to meet him, along with a full bomber flight crew.

As he walked down the line, he shook each man's hand, but when he came in front of me, he paused. He made some comment about us getting older. We were both losing hair. I said, "Mr. President, you look a little tired, maybe you need to get more rest." He said, "Old Sarge, you're right, and I'll take your advice." He reached in his pocket, took out a pen and placed it in my shirt pocket, turned and walked away.

He was not re-elected, but I knew Gerald Ford was a good man and a good president. One thing was for sure — the man who replaced him wasn't half the man he was. Sometimes, when I think of this period when I was at Ellsworth AFB, I take President Ford's pen out and look at it. He had a big heart, this man from Michigan. I will not forget his friendly manner. He loved his fellow man, and was really proud to be the Commander-In-Chief of the Armed Forces of the United States. He had come to office when President Nixon was impeached.

I never did understand why Nixon's people would do their Watergate thing; he was going to be elected in a landslide vote. He had nothing to gain through this stupid thing his people would do. Nixon had made a lot of enemies, and now they would throw him out of office. As it turned out, Gerald Ford was an able replacement, and that morning as I looked at him as he stood in front of me, I thought, "Serve well your country. You were left to pick up the pieces from another person's mistake."

Donna and Pa-a-Sapa

We had come to Ellsworth in 1963, and it was now 1971. Donna was thirteen that year, and we would buy her a horse. She has always loved animals, and especially, horses. The horse was a light blond color, with an even richer blonde mane and tail, and was probably a Palomino and Morgan mix. She had a special name, Pa-a-sapa — which in the Sioux Indian language was "Black Hills Gold". We had an old white pick up Ford truck, which we used to go to the base-owned pasture.

An old dirt road snaked along the top of the plateau where that base was located. Small twisting dirt roads wandered down into the valley below. When the snow came with the howling winds, it was tough traveling along the dirt road on top, much less driving down those little twisting roads to the bottom of the pasture.

Nevertheless, the horses needed food, especially when the temperature was below zero. Sometimes, all the kids would load up in the old truck for the ride. It wasn't long after we started to go to the pasture that Donna would call out her name, and the horse would come running to the truck.

I look back now and realize what a life I was living in the West, and I am sure, now that Donna raises her own family, that she remembers the laughs as we slid along those snow-packed roads, in the old white Ford pick up. It was a time of my life I will never forget. The horse's name was Pa-a-sapa, but to Donna she was always known as Babes.

A B-52 Bomber, Sugar Cane and a Cobra

Utapao, Thailand 1967. My plane had been parked on the end of a taxi-way parking spot. Literally, the jungle was almost on top of us. Sugarcane grew off the left wing, my aircraft had been prepared for the next bombing mission over Vietnam and I was bored waiting on the flight crew to arrive.

I walked down the left wing, checking for anything that might have been missed. I noticed the sugarcane and decided to cut off a piece, peel it, and chew some of the heart.

But, little did I know, someone lived among the sugarcane. His name — King Cobra — and he had to be seven feet long; his head was three feet off the ground. He hissed, and I froze. I was scared to death — at that moment, the crew arrived in their bus. It distracted the cobra; I backed away, took a deep breath and shook all over. I would never eat sugarcane again.

Return to England – 1972

In 1972, I went to England for a bomb competition. Kath flew over to be with me while I was there, and would stay with her brother, Jim. That was when I first got to know his wife, Lorna, and all their lads. Lorna and I had many long conversations about many subjects, not always agreeing, but nevertheless, we enjoyed each other's company and had many laughs. She was top of the line with her great breakfasts — lots of cups of tea, eggs, bacon, fried tomatoes and toast. It made the trip, as they say in England, "grand." We would not return again for fourteen years.

By then, their lads had grown up and Leon, who I played conkers with, was no longer a little boy. Jim, who was a lawyer now, and Lorna with her brain, had accumulated a large amount of property worth a considerable amount of money. All and all, they are now very wealthy — it's said if you live in a park surrounded by stone walls, you can't be poor. We still go back to visit Jim and Lorna almost every year.

In the Fifties, we went to Lorna's mom's house for tea. That would be the day the young boys who would become the Beatles would practice in her back garden. Little did we know who they would become. Lorna's brother, Neil, was their pal and road manager, and still works for the Beatles in some capacity.

When we return now, Jim and I love to go to the races; my favorite racecourse was the steeple chase course in Wales named Bangor-On-Dee. The racecourse, about one and a half miles, egg shaped, was surrounded on one side by a large sloped embankment. There, on the grass, people sat in the sunshine watching the horses jump these giant fences during a race. Before they modernized slightly and built a place for people to eat sitting down, you could buy bacon sandwiches from a portable diner and eat them while sitting on the grass slope. It was an awful lot of fun, and made for a good day out.

One year, we talked Kath and Lorna into going, and they really enjoyed themselves. Jim and I went one year to several racetracks and had a really good time at each, but the best of all was my last trip to Haydock Park. There, in the last race, on a horse named Pass Me By, I won three hundred seventy-six pounds for a twenty-pound bet. It really made my day.

The Little Texan

In 1968, while at Utapao, Thailand, Carl Blackwell, always full of mischief, would play a trick on me that would backfire on him. I had gone to the community shower. Walkways led to the shower from all the hootches we lived in. Boards about eight inches high lined each walkway holding in the gravel in the middle. This was to keep down the mud during the monsoon rains. It was dark, and the pathways were unlit.

Unbeknownst to me, he had hidden and waited for me. I was walking back to the hootch, when all of a sudden this person jumped on my back saying, "Die, GI!" I thought a Vietnamese sapper had slipped in among our hootches.

I bent forward, and slammed him to the ground over my head. As I did this, the momentum carried me down on top of him. He let out a scream. I had fallen on a leg,

117

which was over a walkway board. He was hurting. I picked him up and carried him to the hootch; his leg was black. We then took him to the medical facility, where they x-rayed his leg. It wasn't broken, but was badly bruised.

The next day, he insisted I carry him everywhere on my back, as I was the one who hurt him. You can imagine how funny this looked. He was five feet, four inches tall and weighed 118 pounds. He was from Texas. This proves all Texans are not tall.

Vietnam Sappers — Utapao, 1968

The sound was a sharp click. Then I realized that the gun had malfunctioned. For some reason, I was supposed to live. I looked up just in time to see a satchel charge thrown under the nose of a B-52 that was sitting in a revetment next to the one I was in. A Thai marine grabbed the satchel charge and threw it into the center of the taxiway. It exploded with a roar, and cement flew in all directions. Gunfire broke out all along the flight line; we weren't armed, which made us feel helpless.

Someone in the observation tower overlooking the row of fifteen revetments hit the emergency flood light switch, and the whole area was now lit with the brightest of light. The Vietcong sappers were killed or captured within seconds. We were all happy to be alive.

The next night, while I was enjoying a beer with two Aussie troops, they said to me, "What do you expect, Yank? It's a war zone." Then proceeded to tell me they could penetrate the area without being caught. To prove this, they said they would leave a calling card.

The next morning, when I arrived at my B-52, I found they had stenciled about ten red kangaroos jumping out of an air vent on the side of my plane. They had come through the security patrols without being detected.

Sir, You're Completely Wrong
Ellsworth, 1969

"Attention, you are hereby charged with falsification of aircraft records." I stood there, wondering what he was talking about. I did know something was very wrong. He read all the charges, and then he proceeded to show me several sheets of aircraft records. Each one showed a red cross grounding condition, which had been cleared by me. He then asked whose signature was on each aircraft form correction block. I answered, "Mine, sir."

He then said it had been reported that a large panel had come off an AKC-135 tanker aircraft at Okinawa, and my signature was on the "corrected by" block and the "inspected by" block. An investigation had revealed that I had given my permission to this person who signed it off, to sign my signature anytime he needed to.

At this point I interrupted his statement. "Sir, you don't know what you are talking about. I have been in the Air Force for nineteen years. I would never jeopardize my career like this. Everything you have said so far is false, and if you continue with this, I will demand a public apology when it's over."

He then showed me another aircraft form containing four discrepancies on a B-52 bomber. I had signed three "inspected by" blocks and cleared each red cross. He now pointed to the last block and he asked, "Whose signature is this?" I stated, "It's not mine. That's a forgery." He then said, "The writing expert for the Lincoln, Nebraska Highway Department said it is yours."

Now I knew where I stood, and I wasn't happy. I looked at him and said, "You'd better find another expert. This one is wrong." He said they would do just that. A writing expert at Minnesota University told them it wasn't even close; he couldn't believe the Nebraska expert said it was mine. "You owe the man an apology," said the Minnesota expert.

So, two days later, in the base theater before the entire bomb wing, an apology was read out: "With deep regret, we hereby apologize for a false charge and our conduct to Master Sgt. Billy Marsh." The charges, with an explanation, were then read out. The wing was called to attention and dismissed. My commander came up, shook my hand and said, "Well done, Billy." I had a smile from ear to ear. I had won back my honor.

Guam, 1966-1967-1969-1972

When I first heard we were going to go to Guam and enter the Vietnam War, I must admit I was very excited. This was real war, and I wanted to be part of it. We took off for Guam in early March 1966. As I left that morning, it finally hit me — I'll be gone six months. I will miss my Kathleen and all the kids; just how much, I would learn later.

It was a long flight to Guam. We landed around noon, fifteen hours later. We were stunned to find we were to fly combat missions the next morning. For the next five and one half months, we would launch two fifteen-plane flights each day. The mission to Vietnam was twelve hours total, and made for some long days, near the end of our six month stay.

The pace of bombing would increase. Some days the number of missions was unknown. Two weeks prior to my return to Ellsworth, I was notified that my brother,

James, had been killed in a coal mining accident. I left Guam on a med-evac aircraft out of Vietnam that had stopped to refuel in Guam. After the funeral, I left for Ellsworth AFB, back to my Kathleen and family.

Operation Linebacker

While on Guam in 1972, I was sitting in the snack bar when a colonel with a familiar face walked in. He looked at me and smiled. "Hi, Billy, what are you doing here?" I answered, "Same-o, same-o. Trying to win a war." He said, "Mind if we find a table a little more private?"

We moved to a table by itself in a corner. He then said, "Billy, you've been involved in this since the start. I'll bet you're tired by now." "You've got that right," I replied. He then said, "I'll tell you something, but first you must swear to me you'll tell no one." I swore I would tell no one anything.

He then proceeded, "Henry Kissinger is in Paris, France meeting with Lee-Duc-Toh from North Vietnam. If no peace is agreed upon by the 18th of December, we will then send the B52s to bomb Hanoi." I laughed slightly, thinking this must be a joke. But he assured me this was the plan. I thanked him for his faith in me.

Guam and Utapao, Thailand, 1972

I had been forewarned we would start bombing North Vietnam if the peace talks broke down in Paris, France; the colonel sent to brief the offsets which would be used to get the bombs from our B-52s on target met me by chance in the snack bar on base in Guam. He came over, sat down and said, "Billy, I'm glad to see you," then proceeded to swear me to secrecy. On December 18, we would start the bombing if things did not end before that date.

Now I was with my friend, Charley Bissett. We were sitting in a metro van, monitoring a three-plane cell that was about to start engines. The flight crew was standing by the metro when the radio crackled. "All vehicles, roll call" — all vehicles answered by number. After bomber eleven, I keyed my mike, "Bomber 12 - Roger." Then over the radio came this message: "This is your wing commander. All missions are cancelled. We are entering a period of sustained bombing. All personnel, your full cooperation will be needed and expected. All crews are to report to the briefing room."

We drove to the building. Charley said, "What are you doing? They won't let us in." I replied, "Watch me." We walked to the briefing room and were stopped by a guard. He checked my line badge, but was hesitant about me entering. My wing commander saw me, and waved me in. Charley was impressed.

The briefing started. A curtain opened, and a huge red map of North Vietnam was now visible. "Gentlemen, the target for tomorrow." Deep breaths were heard all over the room — some crew members showed the fright on their faces. The briefing ended with all sworn to secrecy, although the Russian trawler anchored off the end of the runway would know something unusual was up when we launched 150 B-52s at once.

When the launch came the next day, it would take two hours of continuous launching to send them off. After all planes were airborne, Charley drove up to me in his vehicle. He said, "How did you know this was going to happen?" I told him about the officer who had told me a week before. "You knew this, and didn't tell me?" I looked at him and laughed. "I couldn't — it was top secret information."

The first night over Hanoi, we lost six B-52s. The next day we would lose three more. We then went to launching every other day. Much of Vietnam was hit hard. Then, eleven days later, all bombing stopped. We had lost a total of 19 B-52s, North Vietnam had launched 2000 SAM missiles. We would soon go home, but best of all, our prisoners in Hanoi, North Vietnam,would be released and fly home to a great celebration. Only then could we all smile and realize it was all over.

The Cobra, Mongoose and Monkeys

When I returned to Utapao in 1974, many things had changed. The base had modernized to a certain degree. One of the things that had been added was a Friday ritual: In a cage at the beer garden, under a large banana tree, a cobra would be placed each Friday at a specific time. Then a mongoose would be released inside, as well. It was amazing, the attention this battle received. The mongoose, quick as lighting, won 90% of these confrontations.

Set near this cage was a very large cage about ten feet square; inside it lived two monkeys. A GI drinking beer would take a banana tree leaf, place it through the wire cage, and then pour beer down the leaf. The monkeys opened their mouths at the other end of the leaf and would drink cans full of beer, get drunk as skunks, and go crazy. It was hilarious. This only confirms what I've always said, "GIs will do anything for a laugh."

Another thing that was a weekly ritual at Utapao, was a cage had been built with a large cement water hole in the center. A python about seven feet long lived in this cage. The first time I saw him was 1967; a year and a half later, I returned; by now, he was close to ten feet long and had grown at least half his size again.

Every week, a live chicken was placed in the cage. It was unbelievable, but when the python came out of the water, the chicken froze, even when the python would crawl between its legs; but if the chicken moved, the python struck like lightning.

When I went back in 1974, sometimes the chicken would walk around in the cage for days, but now the python was thirteen feet long. I wonder what happened to these animals and snakes, after we left in 1975.

Ellsworth to Alabama, and a Train

We always traveled on a shoestring. These were lean years in the Marsh household. We had left St. Joseph, Missouri and were traveling on a road somewhere between Kansas City and St. Louis. I was extremely tired. It was nearing ten o'clock at night, and I was looking for a place to park.

As we crossed over some railroad tracks, I noticed a small building on the right side of the road. I pulled the station wagon behind the building, facing outward toward the road that circled around the front of the building.

I put Buffy, the dog outside on a chain tied to the door handle. We settled down to sleep. It was a large station wagon; with the two back seats down, and with blankets and pillows, the kids could sleep okay, except

Donna, who always seemed to be unable to breathe with the windows closed. We finally went to sleep.

All of a sudden, a giant light was shining through the windshield and a train whistle sounded. I woke up thinking we were parked on the train tracks, started the car and started moving. The kids were screaming, "You're dragging the dog!" It was pure panic. What had happened?

The train tracks we had crossed prior to stopping for the night wound up the road when the train came around a curve, its light aligned with our windshield. The train engineer blew the whistle because he crossed the road about 50 feet beyond the small building we were behind. We stayed there, dozing with little sleep until dawn, then drove on.

1964-1974
Ten Green Bottles Hanging on the Wall

For many years we would come home on leave to Alabama, which I loved. We would load up the 1961 Ford station wagon, later a Mercury wagon, and still later, a Plymouth Valiant. I would drive for 12 hours before we stopped at a cheap motel for the night; we would take the kids to McDonalds (or whatever cheap place was nearby) for supper, and then watch the news on TV while the kids showered, put them to bed and listen as they complained that they couldn't watch TV all night.

The second day was always worse. Everyone was tired, but we would try to find a place to stop where they could play during lunch. Kath would make up sandwiches from the items we had packed in a cooler. It was a really good time for us all.

We would arrive at James and Ronnie's late in the evening on the third day. But when we got back in the car, after the picnic, we were still 800 miles from Decatur. I would push on until late evening, wanting to get in early as possible to Ronnie's and James' house. We would repeat the cycle from the first night with the kids — sometimes we ate breakfast at a café, if money was OK on this trip.

We were really happy the next afternoon as we crossed over the state line into Alabama. How many times we had sung *Ten Green Bottles Hanging on a Wall* I don't know, but we broke that up by singing *Bunny's Got No Tail At All* or played "I Spy With My Little Eye". I always felt there was some cheating, as there was a lot of whispering between Billy, Judy and their mom, Kath.

We would arrive at James' and Ronnie's, spend the night, and eat all the fresh vegetables and corn bread she could make; plus, she really knew how to make iced tea. Most of the time we stayed for two nights, then, we would proceed to Nick and Gussie's house, where my mom lived. The kids would do many things; Nick was like a big Santa Claus, and had the kids wound up by playing tricks on them any time he was home. My sister Gussie was great with the kids, and was a tremendous cook. She was wonderful to us all, and we will never forget her and, especially, all the drippy chocolate cakes she made.

The Rose Highway

During the mid and late 1960s, we would try to go on leave each summer. It was a long drive from Ellsworth in South Dakota to Birmingham, Alabama. With a car or station wagon full of kids, plus a dog, it was an adventure, especially when we would stop at roadside rest areas. Few, if any, had restrooms. Usually, there was a cement table with a cement bench and a 55-gallon drum for garbage. You had to eat your sandwiches fast, before the flies carried them away. There were very few bathrooms. When we filled up the car with gas, everyone had to visit the bathroom. You never knew when you would see another.

But, as always, we wouldn't be five miles down the road before a voice would start in the back of the car, "Mommy, I have to use the bathroom." They had sworn at the service station they didn't need to go. Finally, we would stop on the side of the road if they needed to tinkle.

Kath told the kids that when we came back along this road, there would be a rose wherever they had tinkled. If that were true, this would have been known as the Rose Highway, stretching from Alabama to Ellsworth AFB, South Dakota.

Al's Oasis

The town was halfway across South Dakota. Chamberlain was really a wide place in the road; it was only called a town because it was one of the largest gas stops as you traveled along Interstate 90. The Missouri River flowed through a valley, with Chamberlain on one side and on the other, high on a hill, a café called Al's Oasis. A large statue of a buffalo could be seen for at least two miles as you approached. On the other side of the valley, a sign could be seen from an equal distance; on it, in large script letters, was "Al's Oasis —Five-Cent Coffee."

When you entered the café, it looked like something out of the Old West. The food was good; the pies, with meringue that stood about four inches high, were awesome. It was hard to pass by without stopping, and we seldom did. Our kids, more than twenty-five years later, still talk about this restaurant.

If you ever go by, it's still there, and the coffee's five cents and you'll never see pies as good, again.

Ellsworth AFB, 1963 – 1976 —
A Look Back

As we drove across the plains of South Dakota, I'll always remember the feeling in the pit of my stomach; although I was pretty self-assured, I still knew this was going to be no picnic. That turned out to be much more true than I had imagined.

In less than five days, I was a crew chief of a B52 bomber. I wanted to be the very best, and to have the best aircraft in this bomb wing. I set out to accomplish this in short order. My ground crew had the same desire. The hours were very long, but in less than six months, we had transformed this bomber into the very best in the 28th Bomb Wing.

Kathleen and our kids were by now starting to settle into life at a remote area of the USA. The first winter was brutal — the cold and snow took a while getting used to, but like all things, your body adjusts and you move on. When I first set foot on the flight line, I felt completely lost, but soon I was settled, and also got to know all the people I worked around. Most of them were friendly, and tried to help me adjust to life at Ellsworth.

Kathleen would meet some English girls and join the British wives' club. The kids would make friends at the community center and at school. In the summer, we camped at Paktola Lake in the Black Hills. What a great time we had. We will never forget our stay at Ellsworth.

We left there in 1976, but even today, as all the kids are now in their forties, except Janet, who has reached the fifties, the base and the Black Hills hold a place in their hearts, as it does in Kathleen's and mine.

1970
B-52 Bomber Crash, Ellsworth AFB

Smoke rose above the base. We had lost the first B-52 in more than fifteen years of flying at Ellsworth Air Force Base. Through heroic efforts by the fire department, all crew members were rescued, but B52 55-058 was a total loss. I would be a member of the crash investigation team.

When I entered the cockpit, which did not burn, I noticed number seven throttle was in the cut-off position. All others were at the one-hundred-percent power position. The pilot had attempted to go around, and missed approach with an engine shut down. He had plenty of power with the other seven engines, but because of uneven power, had let the aircraft drift to the right, corrected, and stalled out.

To the right of the runway, the aircraft settled to the ground, tail first. Landing gears spit out in every direction. The right wing broke off at the wing root. The plane lay in 18 inches of burning fuel. The fire trucks, with total disregard for their own safety, drove through the flames.

A new standard of bravery was set that day. One man on the plane was trapped — the tail gunner. A fire truck rammed the side of the tail until it broke open, and the gunner scrambled onto the hood of the fire truck.

The good Lord smiled on all that day.

The Rapid City Flood — 1972

We could see lightning flashing up in the mountains; it seemed to stay there for an awful long time. Our kids and I loved stock car racing, and were about to enter the gate at the race track, when it started to rain. Not hard, but enough to cause the races to be called off, as this was a dirt track. Little did we know what was happening.

Seventeen inches of rain had fallen in the hills in less than two hours. The water gathered in all the small valleys, then roared into the large valley leading to Rapid City. Without warning, a wall of water arrived in the city below. Part of the town was destroyed in minutes.

Two hundred, seventy-two people died, and except for some heroic rescues, many more would have joined them. A flood plain was declared, and no homes could be built in this area.

The town has progressed greatly since this tragedy. The people who lived here during this time will never forget the sadness which prevailed in this little town.

The Best of the Best

He came to our base at Ellsworth, South Dakota. When I first saw him I remember my first thoughts were, *my goodness, he's young*. He was tall, probably 6 foot three or four. His uniform fit him perfectly. He was one sharp colonel. I said to one of the guys, "How old do you think he is?" He said, "Maybe thirty-six." I shook my head; *boy, they're making them young these days*. I found out later we had missed it only by a year. I was to find out a little later that age didn't matter. This guy was smart. Not only that, he was a leader. Yes sir. This was some good officer.

He had only been our wing commander for a month or so when one night, as we struggled to ready a B-52 bomber for a morning flight, a staff car drove up in front of the plane. He spoke to one of the young airmen, "Who's in charge, son?" "Master Sergeant Marsh," he answered. "Tell him to come to the car." I walked over, not knowing who it was. He said, "Get in." I climbed into the back.

I realized it was Colonel Lawson. He said, "Tell your people to get in." I started to tell him we had a lot to do if this plane was to fly in about seven hours. He assured me things would work out. "Besides," he said, "Do you know how cold it is outside?" I said, "I have seen a lot worse." I looked at him. "How cold is it, anyway?" He said, "The chill factor is thirty one degrees below zero."

He said to one of the young airmen, "I think there's donuts and hot coffee in the trunk." The kid brought around two thermoses, one cream and sugar, one black, and two dozen donuts. Colonel Lawson made this comment, and it stuck with me, "Supervisors must never show that they have any doubt things will work out." I thanked him, and then said, "Let's go fix this bird."

He was our commander for only one and a half years. He would move on to Washington as Nixon's aide. Not too many years later, he was a three star general. I only had contact with him one other time after he left. When I called him, he remembered me, and did what I asked. He was a tremendous person.

RAF Marham, 1972—US and British Bombing Competition

In 1972, while stationed at Ellsworth AFB, I was honored by being selected to form a team of maintenance men and take a B-52 to Britain, to win a bombing and navigation trophy we had never won. I accepted the challenge with great pride — as for myself — I held the highest skill level as a 43191E. I had also been a master crew chief for eight years. We had a motto in our wing: "We are the world famous 28th — non is equal."

—The Contest —

To fly low-level and high-level bomb runs and close tolerance navigation runs. The over-all winner in this competition would win the Blue Steel Trophy. This we did. The British were not happy; when we drank beer from their trophy, they were livid. Sorry mate, better luck next time.

I would leave this competition, return to Ellsworth, celebrate the winning of the Blue Steel Trophy, then head for Guam. But things were about to happen and I will never forget them. Although I had been tired of all the trips, lasting six months each time, I nevertheless was glad I was in the last action against North Vietnam. When it was over, everyone was happy. Most of us went home shortly after the last missions were flown.

Christmas

Christmas was celebrated in a big way in the Marsh household. Kath was, and still is, one of the best Christmas shoppers ever. She always seemed to be able to find just the right things for all the kids and grandchildren. Christmas at our house was the best of times. We always decorated the tree beautifully; packages were piled all around the base of the tree. Late at night, we would see that each child's toys were placed where they would know who they belonged to.

But one Christmas, in South Dakota, at Ellsworth AFB, Judy woke up early, went downstairs and moved Donna's doll and tea set to her pile of toys. I guess she thought Santa brought her two of everything and none for Donna.

One time at Westover AFB, we were flat broke. We went to Sears and asked for a charge account. After two days, they approved it — $250. Seemed like a lot of money, then. We bought the kids toys and a big metal dollhouse. I was still awake, putting it together, at five o'clock in the morning Christmas Day. Kath and I finished everything minutes before they woke up.

We didn't need anything for ourselves. To see the kids as happy as they were, was all the Christmas we needed.

Utapao, Thailand — 1975
The Fall of Saigon

I stepped outside the hootch I lived in, along with Gary Rice. The sun had been up only a short while. I looked up at the sky, and to my amazement, it was filled with hundreds of airplanes of all descriptions. I hollered at Gary, "Take a look at this." He stepped outside— "What in the world!" he said. We all of a sudden realized that Saigon must have fallen.

The planes were starting to land; one ran off into a ditch, and although no more than thirty people should have been on this aircraft, I counted 130 men, women and children as they exited the aircraft. Many were still armed; we took all the guns, knives, and grenades. By twelve o'clock, ten thousand Vietnamese had arrived. They would later be flown to the USA and dispersed throughout the United States.

To say that the people who had served during all these years of the Vietnam War were unhappy, doesn't cover the anger and disappointment they felt. Many tears were shed by those who had lost friends in this war, and a feeling of betrayal was felt by many.

We received notice that all B-52s would be going home in a short while. A week later, the last of the B-52s flew a low-level salute to all the personnel. Two weeks later, we were on our way back to the States.

Utapao, 1974 — Sir, I Can't Do This

Sir, With All Due Respect, I can't do this. The written order said, "All people who are involved in the Drug Program, will be assigned day shift duty only." I felt this was an infringement on my rights as an NCO and member of the armed forces of the United States. I had refused to obey a written order in writing, and as the clerk typed the letter, my supervisor, Chief Master Sargeant McClanihan said, "Billy, be careful. Remember, you are refusing a written order, and doing it in writing. You could have a hard time with this, if the colonel pursues with legal action. You may have technical merit on your side, but he has the uniform code of military justice on his." I looked at him and said, "Mac, I just can't obey what I conceive as an unlawful order."

Now it was to be a battle of wills. When the colonel picked me up in his staff car on the flight line, his first word was a threat, as he was so mad he could hardly talk. I could tell he wanted me to back down from my refusal; I said I had work to do, stepped out of the car, saluted and walked away. I heard the car door open behind me. He almost ran to catch me; he said, "I may have to court-martial you." I looked at him, my anger was now showing through. "I wouldn't do that, you'll lose, and it could hurt your career.", I replied. He went back to his staff car and left.

The young airman who was the cause of all the mess continued to use his drugs, and in less than ninety days, was discharged from the service. On the day I left Utapao, Col. Rue shook my hand, smiled, saluted, and said, "Keep up the good work." I looked into his eyes, smiled and walked away, never knowing what his thoughts really were.

The Bridge, Thailand — 1975

I had seen the movie, but now I was standing and looking at the real thing, the Bridge over the River Qui. We had left Utapao Thai AFB that morning on a tour bus. When we arrived at the memorial grave yard, where more than a thousand men who had died from torture, hard work and lack of food are buried, my mind just wasn't ready for all the sorrow I felt as I read the headstones.

Most were Australian and English troops. It was not known until after the war that the Fifteenth Air Force would wait until the center span on the bridge was finished, and this would be bombed. That way, the Japanese would continue to need the prisoners to rebuild the span and not slaughter them.

Now I stood here, looking at the bridge. I walked out to the center span, which had been replaced by a German company, shortly after the war ended. The old span still had bullet holes from fighter aircraft strafing the bridge. It was noted the first bridge was wooden, but collapsed because the riverbed was too soft. You could still tell where it was built, about 500 yards downstream. From the new bridge, one of the Japanese locomotives sits on tracks off to the side of the railway lines.

The bridge was still being used when I was there, and the railway stretched for many miles into Burma, built on the backs of some wonderful men.

War Birds Leave
Utapao, Thailand – 1975

Today is the 6th of June, 1975. The first B-52 leaves for the States this day. I am sure some of the men stationed here will be happy, as it will mean they will soon go home. Some will have a twinge of regret, especially those who have been involved in the Vietnam operations for all these years, and for some this is a chapter of greatness coming to a close.

For here on the Gulf of Siam, Utapao AFB, the war was carried out against the North Vietnamese and Viet Cong for seven long years. At 09:00 hours this morning, the first of these proud bombers rolled down the runway, never to return. Even the young crewmembers, who never flew combat missions in Vietnam, must have known they were taking part in a historic event.

As I stood and watched the last B-52 leave on the 8th of June, many memories flashed before my eyes, for here on this sprawling base, I had launched many hundreds of missions against the enemy in Vietnam. It had always seemed the B-52s would never leave, but on this day, as I looked at the empty revetments where they had been parked, this was the end of an era that will never be forgotten by the thousands of men who came here.

"The End"
From the book *Why* – Written in 1975
At the Fall of Vietnam

It is now late June 1975; you by now may have wondered why I wrote this story, and if I have misgivings about making the armed services a career. First, I would like to say I have taken the time to write this book for two reasons. My family, who I love very deeply, has, I'm sure, always thought they knew their dad's every thought, and I'm sure my Kath thinks she knows all my feelings and mannerisms. So for them, I took this time so they might know and understand me better and relive my life over all these years with me. I'm sure as they read this book, they will learn a few lasting lessons on what life really is all about; knowing my kids and Kath as I do, this will only serve to enrich the happiness in our lives.

Do I have misgivings about making the service a career? I can only answer you this way; I had a dream twenty-five years ago. That dream is now almost complete. I have been to so many places, met so many people, had so many friends, and as I traveled all these years, I was a proud man. Right or wrong, I have always felt my country was the champion of freedom for all mankind to look to in their hour of need. I have served my country the best way I knew how in the past 25 years, and now in the evening of my career, how could the people who govern our country make decisions such as have been made this last year? Do they seek to destroy all that has been built by our forefathers? Our country has always stood with its friends; our commitment to humanity has always been complete. The question was, "why?" in the beginning and remains, "why?" in the end.

Utapao, Thailand, May 15, 1975

The *Myaguez*, a merchant ship, had been boarded by the Cambodian Navy in international waters off the coast of Cambodia. This would set in motion one of the strangest sequences of events. An Air Force general decided he could take back this ship with twenty-seven security police. Their deploying point for this endeavor would be Utapao AFB, just a few miles from the island where they thought the boat crew was being held. While proceeding to Utapao, the helicopter they were traveling on crashed, and all were killed.

Now, a change of plans would take place the next afternoon. Ten C-141 and C-5 aircraft arrived at Utapao; out stepped 1,000 marines and a sergeant major with a large white bulldog in a spiked collar attached to a large metal chain. The command, "Attention!" echoed across the flight line, and 1,000 sets of heels snapped together as one. I was more than impressed.

The next morning, a stream of FB-111 bombers, F4C fighters and a mixture of other aircraft, roared above and down our runway. They launched from Tak-Lee Air Force base, and now attacked any bases along the Cambodian coast.

Several hundred marines aboard helicopters attacked the small island off the coast of Cambodia and were met with very strong resistance. Several helicopters were shot down, short of the beach. The marines who did make it to the beach were pinned down. The battle raged for several hours. We were surprised by the stiff resistance. We were out-gunned.

Gunships tried to suppress the Cambodian heavy weapons' fire. Marines were starting to die on the beaches. As a last resort, C-130 aircraft dropped two 15,000-pound daisy-cutter bombs five hundred yards inland from the beaches. This suppressed some of the Khmer Rouge fire. Helicopters swept in with guns blazing; Specter C-130s, with mini guns firing thousands of rounds a minute, sought to pin down the Khmer Rouge. The marines withdrew under heavy fire. Forty-one brave men had died. The ship sailed away. It was a high price to pay for a small ship, but it would let anyone know you cannot hijack a United States vessel on the high seas.

Footnote: If you're ever in Washington D.C., stop off at the Vietnam Wall. You'll find all of these men's names who died, imprinted there, and honored as warriors in the last battle fought in Vietnam. Last, but not least, three men never came home. To this day, they are still unaccounted for.

Retirement—1976

In 1976, at the age of forty-four, and after twenty-six years of service, I would retire. We came to Jacksonville, Florida that January and would live on the west side of town until August. Then, we would buy a house in Orange Park.

The kids would all marry in due time, and from these marriages came ten grandchildren. Janet, our oldest daughter, gave us our first grandson. She named him Christian. Debbie would give us Justin and Jessica. Donna, who was not going to have any children, gave us three beautiful granddaughters named Rachel, Sarah and Megan. Judy gave us our first granddaughter, named Andrea, and a grandson named Christopher. Billy, Jr. would give us a smiley-faced little girl named Jordan.

Billy would also have a stepson named Jared, who fit right into the family. Needless to say, we are very proud of our children and grandchildren. We now look forward to great-grandchildren. It is now August 29th, 2005. I have been retired for twenty-eight years. I feel very fortunate to have enjoyed my retirement and all my family over all these years. The years have gone by quickly, but we have enjoyed them all.

Davy Crockett and the Awayo

Christian was four years old the year I went out to Dallas, Texas and helped them move to Orange Park, Florida. When I arrived in Dallas, the temperature had been over 100 degrees for 41 days. It was roasting. I remember Christian taking me down to the lake the next morning, walking along the bank of the lake; I asked how deep it was. He assured me it was shallow and they swam there all the time. I stepped off into the water — I sank underneath. It must have been 25 feet deep. He was jumping up and down on the bank, laughing.

We loaded the truck, and several days later, headed for Florida. It was a long ride, and with no sleep, we arrived exhausted. The Shipp family was moved in, and for the next few years, we became one family. Our fireplace in the den had large gravel around the base. Christian used this to build his fort. He had lots of men from all different games, including soldiers.

We played Davy Crockett and the Defense of the Alamo. We would prepare for battle. I always had the worst soldiers, some without arms or heads. If I started to win the war, he would hide Davy Crockett under the rocks. This didn't make too much sense, but neither did the game.

As I attacked, I would hum the death song. He would beg me, "Please don't sing the death song." I believe in Spanish it was called, *The Awayo*. He would ask me, "Papa, I know you'll say no, but will you please play Davy Crockett with me?" Each night, I found it hard to refuse. After all, one day when he grew up, this would be one of his favorite memories.

Orange Park, Florida – 1976
Billy, Marti, Jordan and Jared

When I retired in 1976, the family came to Florida. Billy would go to school at Orange Park High. He took up wrestling. One night, they were wrestling a team named Palatka. Billy was wrestling a very good wrestler, who almost had Billy pinned. All at once, Billy reversed the wrestling hold and pinned his opponent. He must have jumped five feet high with his arm extended skyward. I thought Rocky had arrived.

Billy went to work at Jewelcor with his mom part time. Then, after graduation, he went to work for UPS and drove the brown truck. He married Marti and became an instant dad to Jared. Billy and Marti had a little girl named Jordan. She is beautiful, loved by all our family and has a lot of Marsh in her makeup.

During the summer, all the grandkids gather here at our house to swim and have a great time. Jared fit right into the family. He would come here and the water fights they had were something else. Jordan loved her big brother very much. They have really been good for each other.

Retirement and Grandchildren

I know through the book I've told stories about our grandchildren, mostly when they were young. Christian, our oldest, is now a tall, slim young man. He took his height and some of his looks from his dad, Bob. They have so many similar traits and hobbies. They would go rock climbing, caving and kayaking. For years, Bob built a climbing wall in the back yard and they would have a great time on it and, of course, the other grandchildren would all have a go at climbing this wall. I might add, most times with little success.

He also favors his mom, Jan, and these last few years, he has become very interested in his mom's birthplace in England. He is married to a wonderful young lady named Christine, who has become a big part of our family. They will return from their second trip to England this spring, April 2006.

Andrea, our first granddaughter, is now a twenty-five-year-old beautiful bride. She was married a year ago to John, another welcome addition to our family. She would have most of her dad's ways, quiet and never needing to be around a lot of people, but she would take after her mom in her dark skin coloring. Her brother, Christopher, five years younger, would be the opposite and the image of his dad — red hair and pale complexion, but would have his mom's outward personality. He is now attending college in Colorado, and plans on making the law his career.

Justin, our third oldest grandchild would take after Holt, his dad, in looks and in many of his ways. They'd share their love of fishing and of course their love of baseball, when his dad was his coach. But, his mom wasn't to be left out. She could many times out-fish them both. Jessica, Justin's younger sister by two years, was his little shadow for many years. They were best friends. Her dad would also be her coach in softball all during high school.

Donna would have three daughters. Rachael was born in Jacksonville, Florida in 1989. Her Nana and I went to the hospital. Robbie, Donna's husband and Rachel's father, was waiting for us, as she hadn't yet made her appearance. After a little while, Robbie came down and took us to the nursery. He was so proud, and there she was under the heat lamp. She looked like her mom — all dark hair, but she is now sixteen and takes after her daddy a lot in looks and height. She is a great teenager, studies hard and makes good grades. She swims on her high school swim team, and has won many ribbons and medals. She also loves to play the piano.

Sarah, her younger sister was born in Jacksonville in 1994. We also had to wait for her to arrive. When we first saw her, she was being held by her daddy, Robert. He was so proud. Sarah is now eleven years old, and is going to be tall like her dad and she has his great big smile. They are so funny together. Sarah plays the cello, is an "A" student and also swims.

Another five years would go by and then our youngest grandchild would arrive, Megan. She was almost a strawberry-blonde. Rachael and Sarah would hold her right there in the hospital room. She was just a real live doll for them to love. Megan is a bundle of energy — she plays non-stop. She also took after her daddy, with fair complexion and blonde hair, though Jim's hair has a little more gray (sorry, Jim). She loves school and also makes good grades. She also swims and plays the violin.

Jared, who is now 20 years old, became part of our family when he was five years old. Billy Jr. would marry Marti and become an instant daddy. They loved each other very much. I remember Kath and I going to the ballpark to watch him play little league ball. Billy coached him several years. They had a great time. During the summer months, Jared and all the kids gathered to have water fights in the pool. He took up wrestling in high school. He was an excellent student.

In 1995, Marti delivered into our lives a little baby girl named Jordan. She would be our only Marsh grandchild, ha, ha. What a bundle of joy she was. Of course, her Nana and I said she looked just like a Marsh. She was born in Orange Park Hospital and she would certainly become a daddy's girl. We were there in the hospital when Billy stood holding her with a great big smile from ear to ear. He was one proud daddy. She is now ten years old and looks like her mommy. They love to go to the movies together and read Harry Potter books. Jordan is an "A" student and takes an active part in her school sports. She is also a swimmer. When she was only seven she would amaze us by how she could dive to the bottom of the pool in the deep end to retrieve toys.

Love you all — end of story — Nana and Papa

Retirement and Grandchildren, II

In 1976, after twenty-six years in the Air Force, Kath and I retired and came to Florida. Most of our children would soon follow. Christian, our first grandchild was born in Kansas City and would be tall and slim like his dad, Bob. But also, had a lot of his mom Jan's traits.

Our second grandchild would be Andrea. She was born in Lead, South Dakota, and she was beautiful. She took that from her mom, Judy with just a little touch of Dan, her dad. Christopher would come along a few years later but in his case he would look like Dan with his red hair, but also had some of his mom in him. He is now studying to be an FBI agent.

Justin, our third oldest grandchild, was born in Jacksonville. He would be, in many ways, like both of his parents, Holt and Debbie. He loves to laugh and fish. Jessica, our second granddaughter, was born in Orange Park. A great sense of humor and extremely smart, she has lots of both of her parents in her make up. Rachael was born in Jacksonville and she would have the looks of her mom, Donna, and her dad. She loved to compete in swimming, but best of all she is a great student in school. Some of that is from both Donna and Robby. Sarah, the cello player, was born in Jacksonville. You could say it in many ways, but she is beautiful. She gets this from her dad, Robert, and her mom. She is also a terrific student in school. Megan, the bundle of energy, quick to learn, quick to do anything, plays the violin, but can be almost anything she wants to be in athletics. She was born with a natural talent. She is also a very good student. A lot of that comes from Jim, but some from her mom Donna as well.

Our only son Bill's daughter, smiley-face Jordan is smart and loving to everyone, has a great personality, swims like a fish, what more could you ask, also, a very good student. She looks like a Marsh with just a tinge of Marti. Last, but not least, Jared, our fourth grandson, has been a terrific big brother to Jordan and she loves her bubba. He's one smart kid and while growing up, played baseball and wrestled. He will soon, I believe, start to continue his education.

I Love You, Nana and Papa and We Love You, Too

When you look at a little bundle of baby when they're born, your first thoughts are what a wonderful miracle this is. Then, you whisper under your breath, "Welcome to our world little lady, do you know how happy we are that you're here?" In a few short years, she would start to grow into a smart little girl. We noticed right off that Jessie wanted you to know she loved you. When she was six years old and had surgery in Shands Hospital in Gainesville, Florida, some of the Gator football players were visiting the children's rooms. One of the players said to Jessie, "Here's my little Gator Girl." She looked at him and said, "Gators, I hate them, Roll Tide!" That was her Papa's team and if it's good enough for him, it's just right for her.

We would watch her grow up in school. She played softball, which we enjoyed, but most of all we wanted her to excel in school, which she did. She would go on to college and today works and goes to school. Her Nana and Papa take great pride in her drive toward success. She is now studying to be a nurse. That's her desire, and with all her caring for her fellow man, she will make a great one.

Play Ball

You could always tell if Justin was pitching. You couldn't find his Nana. She would be hiding behind the dugout. She just could not stand the pressure of watching him pitch. The sounds of kids at little league parks have been a tradition for many years in our family. We would wear t-shirts with Justin's number on them. He was our hero from six years on. We were always at the ballpark when he played. It's really amazing the love that is poured out to children during games.

Although Justin was a good little league pitcher, it was soon discovered that his niche as a ball player was as a catcher. He was always smooth with his set-up and quick release when throwing to bases. His first love would turn out to be fishing and baseball would take a back seat to a rod and reel. He never got tired of chasing the big reds and bass. He and his dad loved to do both of these things together, although his mom, Debbie, loved to fish as well. He would get married and this would slow down some of his hobbies. But, I'm sure he will do all these things with his children as the life cycle repeats itself.

Pete Rose—1980s

The Montreal Expos were to play their farm team, the Jacksonville Suns. I was assigned as one of the umpires in the fourth inning. Pete Rose, playing left field, came running in to make a shoestring catch. The ball was sinking fast. He dove for the ball; trapping the ball, he came up with it in his glove. I jumped straight up, arms outstretched, palms flat down, yelling, "No catch"; the runners on base were running.

Rose came up and threw a strike at home plate. The runner was out.

Coming to bat that inning, he said, "You know, I'm a super star. You should give me that catch." I said, "Except for one thing. You didn't make the catch." He only laughed. I asked if I could get his autograph. He said to come into the dressing room after the game. I gave him two game balls in the dressing room. He took one of the balls around and got the team to sign it. Then he came back and signed both balls and gave them to me. I wished him luck. He shook my hand and said, "Thanks for a good game."

Later that year, I was called to fill in for an injured umpire in a Southern League game. The game ended 1-0, with the Suns winning. The game still stands as the fastest game played in Southern League history — one hour and twelve minutes. I had a great time umpiring.

Eliza Jane — 1900-1990 — My Mom

She told us many stories about her life and the lives of her family. Originally from Birmingham, England, her family would immigrate to the United States in the late 1800s.

In 1900, she was born in Mississippi. They moved to Kansas City when she was a little girl, and traveled across the Midwest by wagon. In a small town in Kansas, one of her extended family members, by the last name of Reed, would gain notoriety as a sheriff and a gun fighter. Some of his life story would appear in a book Zane Grey wrote about the Old West.

Sometime in her childhood, they moved back to the South. While visiting one of her relatives when she was young, she met my dad, who had returned from World War I. They were married soon after.

Shortly after they were married, the Depression hit, and for years she never knew where the next meal would come from. My dad was working in a coal mine for fifty cents a day. These were the years when people made meals from poke salad and wild onions. If you had an egg to scramble with these greens, you were blessed.

I remember when the ladies of our community saved cow feed sacks, which were, printed cotton fabric. It took two to make a dress, and they would trade sacks to get two of the same print. Our clothes were washed in a tub with a rubbing board, using octagon soap cut up into small pieces. You didn't live during this time – you survived.

When we moved to the farm at Sibleyville, with a great garden and raising our own pigs, a beef yearling and chickens, life improved greatly. I remember many times after school, we would almost have a war between us boys as to what daily

program we would listen to on the radio —
The Lone Ranger, Red Rider or Hop Along
Cassidy. I'm sure my mom thought we were
awful. Our connection to the outside world
from our farm was a Philco Radio with a 400-
hour, 9-volt battery.

At about six o'clock, mom would start
supper. She made great biscuits and with
chicken and gravy, it was awesome. If we
didn't have chicken, sometimes we had
sugar-cured ham slices fried, and then she
made red-eye gravy. It was so good. She
didn't need much to make a meal. The farm
supplied most of what we needed.

Mom had a real sense of humor and
loved to laugh. She had twenty-one
grandchildren and loved them very much.
She would have numerous great
grandchildren. She was loved very much by
all who knew her. We moved to Gardendale
in 1948, and in 1950, my dad would die. My
mom was hurt deeply. She would live on in
Gardendale with my sisters and their
husbands. Then, in 1966, the first of her
children would die. She loved James greatly;
he died in a coal mining accident at the age
of 39. A few years after, Herman died in
Mobile, Alabama. She had now out-lived
two of her children. She once said to me,
"Nothing hurts like seeing your children die."
If she had not had her strong faith, I don't
know if she could have survived, but she
would, until age ninety, in 1990. With our
daughter Janet at her side, singing her

favorite hymns, she told my mom, "It's okay to leave us now. Gus, James and Herman are waiting for you." She left here smiling.

Post Script

One day while riding a go-cart on a dirt road in Middleburg, where they lived, Jessica, Holt and Debbie's daughter, was almost killed by a driver speeding right at her. She was seven years old; and this is what she told us — her granny appeared in the middle of the road, and with her hand out-stretched shouted "Stop" and the vehicle stopped immediately. When she left, I guess she didn't go too far, after all.

Our President

When he came to power as President of the United States, this country was at its lowest ebb in my lifetime. The man who occupied the White House was not only a weak president, who was afraid to stand up against the evil empires around the world, but was, in fact, in a job he wasn't qualified for. Never in history did we need a strong president so badly. When I first heard he was running for President, I laughed — a movie actor as the President. Surely this is a joke. As

I said before, we had a weak President in the White House. Now it could get worse.

But I was soon to find out this man who was an actor was also a patriot. He loved his country, and set out to re-establish what this country was all about. He would meet opposition from those who were faint of heart. One crazy even tried to kill him.

He formed a plan to strip Russia of its power. All over the world, and in Washington, many people thought his actions might lead to war. But when Russia tried to intimidate him, he would not back down. He spoke out for any insurgency against Russian rule throughout the world, and encouraged their actions. He built up the US armed forces to the point that Russia was facing a bankrupt government as they tried to keep up. Finally they realized it was impossible and when a new leader took over, he first tried a little heavy-handed tactics, but soon realized he was facing a man who would not give in.

When he stood at the Berlin Wall and said, "Mr. Gorbachev, tear down this wall" the world shook. He had won freedom for millions throughout this world – even the Russian dissidents in prison were freed. Now the world realized what a great man Ronald Reagan was.

I remember as he was sworn in, the hostages in Iran were freed. They understood he was a serious president. The world soon understood as well. He, like all presidents, could only be president for so long. Some fairly good presidents followed him, and except for sweet William from Arkansas, they have done a fairly good job. A few years ago, after a long life, the tall man who stood in the White house for eight years and led us back to greatness, closed his eyes and went home. Only then did we all realize how great he was.

Vernon and Betty

The first time I met Vernon was at a ballpark. That was more than twenty-five years ago. His love of softball had started long before I knew him. It was amazing how jovial he was. He just loved softball and all that went with it. He had started with a lower classification team but he yearned for the day when he would have a team that could compete for national titles.

It all came together one year, when his girls' team won a national championship, and that same day his men's team won as well. He was one proud man. We had a common bond, as I was an umpire and he was a team sponsor. The name Vernon in softball stood for excellence; you will never meet a more friendly or generous man. He was always ready to help anyone. They say that the good die young, and he was a great example of that.

Who would have ever thought my friendship with Vernon through softball would lead to a wonderful friendship between Kathleen and Betty, Vernon's wife. That friendship started over seventeen years ago and has continued to blossom over all these years. When Vernon left this earth, Kath was there for Betty, and Betty has always been there for Kath. She never forgets birthdays and other special occasions, and she is very much like Vernon with all her love. They say that friendships sometimes fade, but I doubt this will ever happen with these two. They like to talk and laugh. Sometimes some friendships are good, and some are great— this is one of the great ones.

The Day Innocence Died

The phone rang. It was my son Billy. He said, "Dad, turn on the TV, a plane just hit the Trade Center in New York City." I had never thought about those two huge towers, but when I turned on the TV and saw what happened, I knew something was very wrong. I first thought something had happened to the pilots aboard the planes, maybe they had blacked out for some reason. But no one knew that in these planes were the most vile people on this planet. Their mission was to crash two planes into the Trade Center buildings.

I sat there in shock wondering, "Who would do such a thing to other human beings?" But at this moment we didn't realize what sub-humans we were dealing with. I could not accept that anyone could do this. But when the first tower collapsed, my mind went blank. *Dear God, this can't be happening.* Then it was reported the Pentagon had also been hit by a plane and another might be hijacked, and headed to Washington DC. We were under attack by hostile individuals; this was war on our country, pure and simple.

In months to come, the people of the United States rose in righteous indignation to find and kill those who did this cowardly act. The USA went after anyone even remotely connected to this act of terror, but soon the first grumbles of "You're overreacting," were heard. Within two years, we were now starting to be accused by other countries of being bullies and murderers. War was not a proper word when dealing with terrorists.

By 2005, we were now the bad guys. It was the start of Vietnam all over again. The Democratic liberals were accusing our men of murder in Iraq, even though they were using every dirty tactic to kill our men and their own people. But still the liberal media said all this was our fault (sounds like Vietnam again). I find it very strange that you see terrorists all over Iraq firing off their guns and our news people filming this and giving them all this publicity. In wars fought by this country prior to Vietnam, this would have been called collaborating with the enemy. Does anyone ever wonder why terrorists let you film what they do, except to use it for their own purposes? Now that they have tied the President's hands, he is extremely limited in what he can do. Today is the twenty-first of June, 2006. Did 9-11 happen? It must have been a dream, otherwise I wouldn't hear the liberals crying "surrender" again.

Christopher — June 7, 2005

Dear Christopher,

Great hockey player, great golfer, great red-on-the-head, great student and also great-grandson of my Dad, who was also great.

Now that I have used most of my great words, I'll go on to say how proud I am that you have excelled as a person. Most people can go through life just getting by in all things. It's very obvious this is not your life's plan. I'm sure you will do well in your college studies, as I'm sure you know this will decide what you qualify for in the every day world of competition for the best of jobs. Always remember, don't settle for second best. Reach for the gold in life as with all other things. You may not always be first, but if not, you'll be so close it doesn't matter.

Life's good — wear it with a smile.

Love, Papa

Christopher

I guess most kids have a hero, and for Christopher, his was Justin. When he came to Florida on his vacations, his first love was to watch Justin play baseball. It wasn't the only thing he loved to do, but I always noticed he would go on the field after a game and run the bases with Justin chasing him, trying to tag him out.

He was your typical little boy, wound up and ready to play any game. He also had this love for fishing and when we would go on vacation to Fort Myers, Florida, he and Justin would fish every day, between swimming and playing on the beaches. They had some great summers together over the years.

He would grow up, graduate from high school, become a really great hockey player and in his senior year, they would win the state championship. He was thrilled beyond words, but, probably no more so than his dad and mom. Today, you'll find him in Northern

Colorado College with an ambition to be an FBI agent. With his will to succeed, I have no doubt he will be just that.

The Three Great Swimmers

After mastering the art of swimming, these three sisters would move on to become musical artists. Their names would become famous. First there was Piano Rachel, then Cello Sarah and lastly, Violin Megan. Each in their own way would excel in most everything they would attempt. Each one would demonstrate a passion and compassion for most everything. Each one is a reflection of what their mom and dad were like, with just a little dash of their Nana and Papa's love and spirit. The screams of "Go Rachel, Go – Go Sarah, Go – Go Megan, Go" was the rallying cry by the family at all the swim meets.

We all beamed with our love and how proud we were for their efforts later, as they played their musical instruments at concerts. Your heart melted as you watched them play. It may have not been perfect, but it was, to their family's ears. Last, but not least, we know you will always make us proud. We promise we will try very hard to do the same for you. So from all your family, we say "Go Rachel, Go – Go Sarah, Go – Go Megan, Go – Play on – Play on."

Andrea

The phone rang. Dan was on the phone from Lead, South Dakota. Our first granddaughter was born. Kath and I packed our suitcases, and took off driving to their home in Lead. We had stopped at a motel on the way there, and Kath was talking to Judy on the phone; Judy said her name would be Andrea. My answer to that was, "I don't care what they call her. I'm calling her 'Puddin' Face'", and I did. That nickname stuck with her to this day, although I don't use it like I once did.

She is just too pretty. But, she had that cute little fat face when she was born. In the years afterward, as she visited many times, we used to sit on the steps and eat Bama pecan pies and drink Nehi orange drinks. We also used to head for the donut shop on many occasions, all the donuts she wanted to eat, and any drink she wanted. These are the memories I'm sure she and her Nana and Papa will never forget.

My Sister Gussie

We always looked forward to our vacations when we were in the Air Force. We would load up and head for our families in Alabama. My oldest sister, Gussie, would greet us with hugs, kisses and a wonderful welcome, not to mention, the fantastic cakes she would bake. She was a supreme cook. Her love for us was unconditional — the kids still talk about her letting them eat ice cream for breakfast. Her husband, Nick, loved us all and would do anything for us. I will not forget the thousands of games of Rook we played, I still laugh when I think of Nick trying to hide the fact he had the bird as we played this game over and over.

He died in a tragic bus accident. Our mom lived with Gussie most of her later life, and we owe a lot of thanks for what she did. Gussie and Nick had three children. William, who served his country in the Army, married and had two children. He died tragically at a very young age. I will always remember Nick for all the time he lived with us at Sibleyville when he was a little boy.

Judy, her oldest daughter married Joe and they would have three children. Jackie, her other daughter, lives in Birmingham near her mom. Gussie would marry a really good person named Preston. He loved and looked after my mom faithfully for many years, for that I am very thankful. They now live in Tarrant City, and I guess that's their final move. I guess you could say they're home.

The Marsh Body Shop

They had a tremendous reputation, not only as good people, but also for repairing automobiles. The whole family worked for the company — brothers and grandkids, they all made up the company called "The Marsh Body Shop." I never did figure out who started or owned this company. They all shared in the work, and as the company grew and more Marshes were added to the workplace, each taught one another the finer points of repairing damaged vehicles.

This family was the offspring from my brother, James and his lovely wife, Dorothy White. They, like most families who lived in and around Warrior, Alabama, would live from payday to payday. But, as the sons and daughters of this family grew up, they would seek out more opportunities for a better life.

This led them into jobs in Birmingham, one of which was the repair of damaged automobiles. They would build their own business, and today enjoy a fair amount of success. I'm sure they would tell you they are the best at this type of work, and I'll admit, they are really good. Some say they are a great family and except for one small character flaw (each is a devout Auburn University football fan) they really could be good.

Mobile, Alabama — 1960s — The Bottomless Creek

Kath and I would come to Alabama almost every year on leave from South Dakota, where I was stationed in the Air Force. Sometimes we went to Mobile to visit my next-to-oldest brother, Herman, and his family. One day, he told his and our kids he was going swimming in a creek nearby. All the children wanted to go. Arriving at the creek, he dove in with his dog, Lady, following right behind him. He swam back to where the kids were now standing. "How deep is the water?" they asked. He said, "Not too deep, but that's not what you should worry about."

Then he told them this story about a family that came here to swim one day. One of their young boys dove in, but didn't come up. The mother dove in; she didn't come up, either. The sister dove in and she also didn't come back up. Becoming alarmed, the father dove in and he stayed down as well. They were never heard from again.

But, the story goes, if you swim down too deep, they will reach up and pull you down with them. This has to be true, after all, it was told by my brother, and Herman never lied — would he??

You Can't Fish Here

My brother Herman loved to fish. After he suffered a heart attack and became disabled, this was one thing he would enjoy. He really knew how to fish, and lived in the perfect place, as Mobile Bay was only about a mile from his house. Several rivers ran into the bay and this caused the water to be brackish, so in the bay, you might catch any type fish.

I remember one time, traveling up a river just a short way and using a fly rod and top water fly, we caught a large coke-box, full of very large bream. We had a fish fry that evening. He loved to cook these fish and could eat at least ten of these large bream.

Herman really loved his fellowman. But, one day while fishing with Edgar White, they were catching a lot of fish and another boat came up near them. The stranger kept getting closer, until he was right on top of them, and had moved so close, his fishing line had tangled with theirs. Herman then asked him to move. His reply was he could fish where he liked. Herman said, "Not in that boat you're sitting in." Then he proceeded to take his shotgun, and shot the front end off the other boat. It sank in minutes. They took the fisherman to the causeway and then returned to fishing. Strange to say, no police ever showed up.

My Brother James and His Family

Strange, how families form close friendships. Who would have thought that the love of football would have forged the bond I have with my oldest brother's sons. In football season, it's almost a daily ritual that we call each other. Auburn and Alabama — can it get any better? When recruiting season arrives, it's a totally different game. Who would get the best players? One thing I've never mentioned, although I never asked him, I feel James could have been an Alabama fan.

I remember how he would look at me. He didn't know exactly how to express his love for you; it was almost as though he felt he wasn't worthy to say those words, but I know James Marsh loved everyone around him, and so did his loving wife, Dorothy. Sometimes he spoke in absolute jest about many things. Dorothy would say in her slow, southern way of talking, "James, you don't mean that." It was almost as if their whole life had one purpose, and in the next page or so I will try to write what that purpose was.

Their first son, Dennis, who today is 61 years old, married Labreska, and they have two children, Dennis Jr. and Kelly and four grandchildren — Eddie, who is fifty-nine and married Gail and they have three children;

Eddie Jr. Gayla and Stacy and eight grandchildren. Jeff married Rena and they have two children. Brandy, who married Jerry, and they have three children, Haley, Avery and Allie. Matthew, their son will marry Kelly while this book is being written. I'm sure they will add to the Marsh clan. Sandra, the only daughter, would marry Donnie. They would have two children, Jamie and Josh and three grandchildren. Ronnie married Margaret; they have two children and one grandchild.

This is James and Dorothy Marsh's legacy. They are not here today. James died in 1966 in a coal mining accident; he was only thirty-nine years old. Dorothy would live to the year 2000. She never changed. A kinder person you would never meet. They were two wonderful people. After I joined the Air Force in 1950, I was always gone, and could not share my life with them. Life has many twists and turns. Not all work out the way we like, but one thing I'm sure of — James and Dorothy left their mark upon this earth so that their children would have much better lives than theirs. I'm sure they could not, and would not, ask for more.

Herman and Jean's Family

When Kath and I and our children would come back to Alabama on vacations from Ellsworth AFB, South Dakota, sometimes we visited my brother Herman and his family in Mobile. Their children, Terry, Ricky, Ray, and Myra Fay and my children, Janet, Debbie, Donna, Judy and Billy would have a great time playing together. Herman and I would fish and come back with dozens of fish. We would then have a great fish fry. You could not have a better time.

Herman was a really great person. Jean, his wife, always made us feel more than welcome. We have lost touch over the years, but we still have a lot of good feelings about my brother's family.

Herman and Jean's oldest son, Terry, married Joan. They would have two children, Cliff and Craig and two grandchildren, Gracie and Noah. Ricky married Denise and they would have two children, Heather and Keith. Myra Faye would have a wonderful family of four children. Tragedy would strike the family when the second child, three-year-old Brandon, was killed by a vehicle on the road in front of their house. Brian, Brittany and Derek are now her family and their mom loves them greatly, but she will never forget Brandon.

Jean, their mom, lives on in Mobile. Like all of us, she loved her children and grandchildren. It's been a great journey. I'm sure she loved it all.

Ray and Jackie — 1958

When I left for the Air Force in September 1950, Ray would be the last of the Marsh children at home. Little did any of us realize, in three month's time my dad would die and then all that remained in our household were Mom and Ray.

In a few years. Ray would grow into a stud football and baseball player. When he graduated, he would continue his education and would attain a degree, then continue on to attain a master's degree. He would also serve several years in the Army and was in the Elite Guard at the Capital in Washington DC. He married Jackie and they have two children, Jackie Ann and Joy Lynn. Jackie Ann married David while Joy Lynn married Todd. Between them, they would have four children. This brought much happiness into their families and, I'm sure, into the lives of Ray and Jackie. If you're ever traveling through Alabama, they live in a place called Branchville.

Stop by, and they will make you welcome; they might, if you prod them, tell you a little about their football team and

Auburn University. They are both retired now and enjoying the fruits of their labors. There's not much more anyone can ask of life, I'm sure they would say.

A Strike, a Swing, and a Lost Tooth.

One day in the 1940s, my brother, James, who was the oldest boy in our family, was the catcher in a cow pasture ball game in which we were playing. We had no catcher's mask. He insisted he could catch without one.

We had been playing a while, when a fastball was fouled back straight into his face. When we looked to see how badly he was hurt, his mouth was a mess; and when he opened his mouth, one of the large center upper teeth was missing. It did not stop the ball game, and the tooth was never replaced.

His children, later in life, probably thought he was born that way. James, my brother, was a real good ball player, but was a much better person. We all lost a lot when he died young.

A Great Ball Player — A Great Person

His first words to me were always the same, "Hey Billy, How you doing?" He was a very caring man. In the late 1940s he, along with other men and some young high school baseball players, were playing in a semi-pro league in Birmingham, Alabama. I was one of the youngest men who played on these teams. John Jolly, the man I'm writing about here, was a terrific catcher with a really great arm. You just didn't try to steal bases from him.

He also had that tremendous spirit and fire that made him excel over other players. He always walked to the plate, tapped it once with the white ash 36-inch bat, and looked at the pitcher with defiance. He was fearless, but he was good. We were playing in Rickwood Field in 1948, and facing the best team in the state. He hit two homeruns over the scoreboard in left center field. The balls traveled more than 450 feet.

That same year, playing at Trafford, Alabama with our team, losing seven to zero in the top of the eighth inning, I pinch-hit for a guy, got a hit and started a rally. When the inning was over, I had two hits, scored two runs, and we were now tied. In the top of the ninth, I got up, got another hit and scored. We took the lead, nine to seven. Then, in the bottom of that inning, I made a great catch to win the game. I've never forgotten that day, and I've never forgotten John.

John and Doris Jolly

They lived on six acres of land in Gardendale, Alabama. After we moved there in 1948, we would turn it into a beautiful small farm. Jean, Brad and Mary would be born here. My dad and John would look at everything growing and declare it was the best they'd ever seen. After I joined the Air Force, my dad, mom and Ray would continue to live on there for a few years. My dad would come up to John and Doris' house, get Brad and they would eat breakfast at the little house where he lived. They had a close relationship, and I'm sure he and my mom loved Jean and Mary the same. When my dad suddenly died in 1950, a really good man had died.

John formed a baseball team in the Youth Dixie League. They almost won the state title. Brad played for his dad and he was one proud dad. Jean married Joe and they would have a daughter, Missy. She married Cameron. They live in Georgia. Brad and Peggy would marry and they live outside Birmingham. Mary (Pebbie) married Fred and they would have two boys, Freddy and Parker. They live a stone's throw off I-65 in Homewood. John has left this earth for a better place. I loved John. He was one good man. He now waits for his first love. God bless them both.

A Guy Named Joe

The casket flew open and there he lay, all dressed up in his chief petty officer's uniform, a Bama magazine and Bama cap lying to the left of his head. I almost said, "Hi Joe," but decided to say something more appropriate for the moment. I spoke about the twenty-six years I had known Joe, and over all this time, never won an argument. He was the most stubborn man I have ever known, but he was also my best friend.

He loved Alabama football, and that is what occupied our minds on Saturdays when they played. Sometimes, in close games, he would call and wouldn't let me off the phone until the game was over. This past year, while I was watching Bama play, my thoughts returned to Joe, wondering, "Would he have liked the way things were?" He was hard to satisfy.

When the funeral was over, several people asked me if it wasn't a shock, when I slapped the casket as I illustrated his stubbornness and it flew open. I said, "It should have been." But knowing what he was like, I felt he might be getting back at me, one last time.

Not a Grandiose Church
But Grand People

It was never meant to be a great temple, but if you measured this church by its spirit and worship it would rank with the largest and tallest ever built. They say the people make the church, in this case, I know it's true. Where could you find a person more spirit-filled than Hall Hunt, or a deacon like Roy or Joe Ryan, who was our deacon for many years? How do you play a piano like Charlie, or a guitar like Barbara – Hal-le-lu-jah, or John and Penny looking so happy together? The Akels, all of them, Ellen, Barbara Poremeba, and Nadine always ready to do anything to help the church. Ellen Johns and her family — no task is beyond her energy. Randy Hill, if you're sad, don't go near him; he only has time for a laugh and a smile. The sign keeper, Carliss — Jerry taught her well. Frank and Carol always throw a great Christmas party every year. The crowd who feed and clothe the homeless, and Tom who has done so much with the youth of the church, to those who are working to form a new beginning as we exit the Episcopal church and become Anglicans, to all those not mentioned here — you're all the greatest and we love you greatly.

No — Yes — No — Yes —Maybe

The one thing you could always count on was that the food would be good, and someone would inject some humor in every serious conversation if things got a little testy. During a really serious moment, you would notice Hall's eyes glance up over the top of his reading glasses and things seemed to calm down. Gary always seemed to say just the right thing to invoke laughter when things became too serious. This would in turn set off Richard, who tried to restore order.

Then, one of the few nights I would attend these meetings, the subject concerning cleaning the church carpets became hilarious. Jerry was trying to explain that the same company that had done this work before had done the most recent work, but he felt the cleaning bill was too high. He kept trying to tell the group what this price was, but for some reason just couldn't say it.

Finally, he started to say the price and began with the number four thousand and something. Everyone gasped, thinking the amount was four thousand and some odd dollars. As Jerry continued, he added the word "square feet" (talking about the church's square feet of carpet to be cleaned) and then proceeded with the correct amount of $850.

Jerry's face turned red as he realized what he had caused the committee to think.

After much laughter and gasping for air, they finally agreed it had to be paid, but with some adjustments if possible.

Frank, with his stately gray hair and his combat experience, seemed to always take a straight approach on most discussions. He spoke his piece and let the chips fall where they may, but he was also a warm and friendly person to everyone. I noticed one person in particular never seemed to get excited. Roger, in his own way, would start after everyone had his or her say, "Well, as I see it . . .." If he had finished that with "podner," I would have thought John Wayne had just ridden in. One thing I will say about these meetings, in the end, they always accomplished whatever needed to be done, and always with the best interests of those they served. They are called the "Vestry." But, I call them "Good Samaritans."

The First String Priest

It was New Year's Day, two thousand six. Jerry Ballmann read the lessons, then Roy, the deacon read the Gospel. He waited until Roy set down, then he said, just as the Gospel says, "God sent His Son, Jesus to this earth as a common man. He even gave him a common name, Jesus, which is also Joshua."

Arnie had a way of capturing your attention. You could always depend on him coming up with something totally unexpected in his sermon. This time would be no different. He said in his own way, in the time of Jesus, the Jews were looked down on as the lowest of that society.

Then, out of nowhere, he grabbed our attention when he said his own name was also common. As a matter of fact, his parents had no idea about naming him Arnold, but an uncle had died tragically in their family, and when he was born, he was named after him as sort of solace to the family in grief, even though this name was not his family's first choice

When he came to our church, he was always referred to as the substitute priest, but believe me when I say, he was no substitute. He was first string all the way. His sermon would end, and a short while later the service was over. But he had left his words imprinted on our hearts. Thanks a lot, Arnie; looking forward to next time.

The Altar

Made of plain varnished boards, there is nothing glamorous about its makeup, but for some reason when you kneel at this certain place to pray, you have this awesome feeling what you are about to pray about will be answered in God's own way and in most cases, a positive result for what you're praying about.

I know many times as we gathered here, there was much sorrow to be shared and prayed about. Many times, I'm sure, people knelt in utter desperation feeling that only God's answer to their prayers was the only way out.

I know we have lifted many people up in prayer, and then found out, days later, that unexplained healing has taken place. I'm also sure there are those who doubt that prayer heals and changes people's lives in many ways.

So, I guess if you're around after Wednesday night service, look at the altar rail; you will probably see Hall, Roy, Elizabeth, John, Jerry, Carliss, Arlene, Lee, Frank, Carol and many others I haven't named here, as they pray for those in need of prayer.

To Prison With Joe

I'm not sure about the exact year I started to go with Joe to prison, where he would hold services for the prisoners. But this I do know, it was quite a trip. Joe, with his Irish humor, made things just right.

One Sunday, after clearing through the holding area, as we entered the prison, he was telling me about the first time he came here, more than twenty years before. He said he had lost the notes to the sermon he had spent days getting ready. Blessedly, he remembered a lot of what he had written down, and felt he would do okay. As the prisoners settled down in their pews, he looked out at them, then started with these opening lines, "Greetings, God loves you."

Then he drew a blank. He couldn't for the life of him remember anything else he had written. He said, "I must have said, 'God loves you' a hundred times. That was almost the total sermon." He looked at me and said, "Can you imagine this happening to you?" I said, "Joe, you must have almost died."

We were now entering the little chapel; the prisoners were sitting down in the pews. Joe stood before these men. Then, all of a sudden, he said, "I have a real treat for you guys. Mr. Marsh, a dear friend of mine, is going to preach today's sermon." I had been had by one shrewd character. The complete story was to set me up. He looked at me, then said, "Remember, God loves you." The world was a better place because of Joe Ryan.

The Guardian Angel — 2002

That morning I went to the eye doctor. My appointment was at 8:30. Kathy would leave the house at about 9 o'clock. I had never been seen on time at this doctor's office, but for some reason, at 8:30 I was seen by the doctor and was out by 9 o'clock.

I went to Dunkin' Donuts on the way home. As I got my coffee and a donut, I noticed a friend down the counter. He motioned to me to come down. As I approached him, a voice seemed to speak to me. I first ignored it, thinking I was imagining this, but again I heard this voice — *go home*. I set the coffee and donut down, and said to my friend, "I have to go home." He wanted to talk to me about something, but I insisted I had to leave.

As I approached my house, I noticed a truck parked on the city easement, next to the sidewalk and hedge by my home. I pulled into the driveway. I then noticed the metal gate was open to the right of my car. I had closed it when I left that morning, as it had been left open the night before when I drove the lawn mower through to the lower yard.

I walked over to the gate. I heard something, but I wasn't sure what it was. Looking around the corner of the house, I saw a TV, shotgun, camera, lawn equipment and other items lying on the ground. At that time at the bottom of the yard I could see someone was behind the privacy fence that led out to the road just below where the hedge ended. I asked, "who's behind the fence?" The answer was in a Spanish accent, "Is there a creek back here to fish in?"

I knew then that he was the burglar, and my life was about to be put in real danger. He came over the county fence. At the end of the privacy fence, I saw my pistol in his back pocket. He turned toward me, and motioned toward me, "Come here, man." His voice made me guess he was Puerto Rican. I looked at his truck tag number and memorized it. I knew I was about to be shot. At that moment, the mail lady drove up. I stepped to the right, told her I was being robbed and to let me inside. She said, "I can't let you inside." She then engaged the drive, and I walked slowly up the street with my hand on the window opening. I told her the tag number of the truck. She wrote it on a piece of paper, handed it to me, and then drove away.

I looked back; the robber was getting into the truck. I ran into the house and called 911. The robber got away, but I picked out his picture in a lineup. Everything matched; they had no problem finding him. He took my pistol and robbed a bank in Jacksonville. They chased him for several miles, and then knocked him into a ditch.

A few days later, I was talking to my postman, and I said, "Tell the young lady who took your place on Monday, she may have saved my life." He looked at me. "No one took my place on Monday, Billy. I delivered your mail about twelve o'clock, like always." I stood looking at him. I thought he was joking. Then he said, "We don't have any lady drivers. You might consider she may have been your guardian angel." I know now she must have been.

Oh yes, I forgot — the paper with the tag number was never seen again.

The Donut Shop

One thing I learned really quickly about going to donut shops was that you were going to meet a lot of different people, and most of them had their own story to tell. A lot of humor was passed and shared amongst many people, and so, I must add, was a lot of sorrow. Each person you met had his or her own distinct personality.

When I first met Bill, it was as if I had known him for many years. His slow, thoughtful way of discussing any subject would disarm anyone who had a radical or mean view. On most subjects, he almost always said in his own way, "Well, the Bible says so and so." This would, on many occasions, leave you searching for a reply. Then, he would smile and say, "And that's what I believe."

Although our conversations would cover a broad range of subjects, especially world affairs, the war in Iraq, and other government problems, invariably we would return to our families or wander through some parts of the Bible. His favorite thing was his belief in unity of the churches, that is, the people of all faiths. I always said good luck on that, but I guess if you believe strongly enough about anything, it could happen.

That's why if you see a person sitting in a donut shop, say hello to them. You may have just met a friend for life.

Wreck on Kingsley

As you travel through life, there are literally hundreds, maybe even thousands, of times where you have the opportunity to help and pray for your fellow man, and that goes especially for your children and grandchildren. You should never look to be repaid, but sometimes things happen that make you believe that a divine presence is built up around a person whose life is spent loving those around him or her.

I had come home at a few minutes before five PM. Kath wasn't back from her Wal-Mart run. I thought that was strange, because we were to eat dinner prior to my going to church for Wednesday prayer service.

I had a shower and had just stepped out, when the phone started ringing. I came down the hallway quickly but it stopped ringing. Now it hit me— something must be wrong, maybe the car quit running or something of that nature. Still, I wasn't comfortable.

Then it rang again, and I heard her voice, "He ran the red light and hit me. I'm okay." I said, "That's all that matters." Then she said she would be going to the Orange Park Hospital emergency room. She said the Pathfinder was upside down in the road. I visualized this as I tried to calm her.

Our family has been blessed many times. Her children have always been protected by her prayers, and now, in a time when her life hung in the balance, Jesus reached out and held her close to Him. She had no serious injuries. All her goodness and all her prayers and love for others were repaid that day.

The Dream

I was seventy-four years old and now lived in Orange Park, Florida. When I woke up that morning, I felt very strange. I had not dreamed of my dad for many years. Now, after all this time, it was so real it was as though he might walk through the door any minute. That was the way it was in the dream. I had opened the door and there he was. "Come on in," I said. "You've been away a long time." He said, "Yes, I know." It seemed so strange, looking at him. He still had that wonderful smile.

I said, "Dad, the world has really changed since you were last here." I wanted to explain all the things that had happened since 1950 when he died. I turned on the television just to see his reaction. He was amazed. When I told him pictures could be transmitted around the world by satellite, he really didn't understand. When I told him about the interstate highway system, he didn't call me a liar, but he might as well, after the look he gave me.

There was so much I wanted to show and tell him. I said, "Dad, I was involved in a war that lasted seven years." He asked, "Who was the war with?" "Vietnam," I answered. He didn't know who or where Vietnam was. Then, finally I said, "Dad, it will be hard to believe, but men have traveled to and walked on the moon's surface." That's when he said, "That's impossible!" I assured him it had happened.

He looked at me. "Billy," he said. "Did all this really happen?" I looked into his eyes. I could see in his face our Shoshone Indian heritage. His reddish-brown skin was deeply wrinkled. "All this, and many thousand of things too complicated to even explain," I said. "Dad, do you have any idea how many grand- and great-grandchildren you have?" I started to name off each one of them. Then, all of a sudden, I realized I didn't know all their names. He smiled. "It's okay." Thanks for bringing me back."

I glanced at my hands as we hugged each other. They were small, and had no wrinkles; I was wearing overalls, and I must have been about 12 years old. He turned and walked away. I hurried to open the door. It wasn't necessary; he was already gone. A slight smell lingered in the room. It was so familiar. It carried me back to our farm in Sibleyville, Alabama, when I sat on his knee at night and he told me stories.

I know now, this had not been a dream. I had always felt I might be his favorite. My mom said he cried when I left for the Air Force in 1950. He died seven weeks later, and had now chosen me as the one he would travel through time and space to see again — if only for a few moments.

The Hurricane — 2005

As the hurricane approached and swerved over the tip of south Florida, it was a very minimal storm. When it entered the Gulf of Mexico and warmer waters, it at once increased to a Category Two or Three hurricane. No one could envision what was to come. It soon became a Category Four and headed toward the Gulf coast, especially Mobile, Alabama and Gulfport, Mississippi. The storm continued to grow, and would reach Category Five and at one time was above that. Winds were at 175 miles an hour. Now everyone knew wherever it hit, damage and loss of life would be severe.

A day before landfall, the people of New Orleans were advised to leave the city, as the storm had now turned and was heading straight at their coast line. A lot of people did not respond to this warning, and many would die. The storm at the last moment moved about 50 miles north of its track. The main winds then swept across part of South Alabama and ripped apart Gulfport, Mississippi and surrounding areas.

In the meanwhile, New Orleans was hit by a storm surge that caused a failure in their levee system that protected the city. The town flooded. The deaths of people started to mount. It is estimated three years from now maybe, things might be normal. The suffering of these people, this includes all the people affected by the storm, was probably the worst disaster ever in the USA.

The blame for a lot of what went on would be laid at the feet of the federal government. But a lot of the blame should rest with city government in New Orleans and with their governor of Louisiana. You could also say the people did not do what they were told to do. It really doesn't matter, for all that went wrong cannot be changed now. You learn from your mistakes and move on. The response by the ordinary people to all that human suffering was unbelievable. They poured out their hearts to all these people. Semi-trucks loaded with everything needed, rolled into this area of total destruction. Billions of dollars were pledged and given. All of these would be needed, along with government funds, to rebuild the cities and homes affected.

Some say it will never be the same. The loss of income, tourist trade, and the amount of money it would take from the government, will in all probability cause a slowdown in our economy, and in personal income for all people. The price of fuel alone will cause prices to surge, affecting everyone. Disease has now become a real threat not only for the people of New Orleans, but may be contagious, and because people from that area are now spread throughout the country, this could cause a real problem throughout the United Sates. We can only pray this won't happen. We will overcome this disaster, because the Holy One Himself blesses this country.

Roll, Tide, Roll — 1992 Undefeated

In 1992, the University of Alabama football team would go undefeated thirteen wins in a row. The coach was Gene Stallings. In order to accomplish this, he had to defeat the University of Florida and its coach, Steve Spurrier. During the regular season, they'd play, then again and win the conference championship. After accomplishing this, and beating Miami in the Sugar Bowl, they were awarded the national championship.

The state of Alabama went crazy, but on a campus to the east of Tuscaloosa, called Auburn, they were not happy. This would lead to a lot of hatred by several schools, especially Tennessee, and Phil Fulmer. He would almost ruin the university's name, although Alabama was guilty on some of the charges, Tennessee was likewise guilty on many violations. Because they had ratted on Alabama, the NCAA turned their back on all their violations; but, there will be a day of reckoning.

No championship – Auburn 2004-2005. An undefeated 12-0 regular season and a season-ending defeat of a bowl team, Virginia Tech, left Auburn at 13-0 for their season. When they were not picked to play for the National Championship, they were not happy, and I agreed they had been had by the polls. Their greatest season would end in frustration. Most of my family in Alabama were Auburn fans, and for the first time ever, I felt sorry for them. I have waited for many years for both teams to meet undefeated in the last game of the year. They are building two powerhouse teams. Maybe this or next year will be the year.

Warrior — Revisiting My Childhood

On the tenth day of March 2007, I and my wife, Kathleen, along with her brother and his wife Lorna, who were over from England, visited my old school in Warrior, Alabama. The people who taught there were restoring the high school building. I was shocked to find the principal of the school on a scaffold, painting the gymnasium. It was a labor of love for this man. He told us the plan was to tear down this building and he refused to allow that to happen. The building structurally was very sound. The floors were all hardwood. The building, built of red brick, was in great shape.

The principal took us on a tour of the school. I told him my teacher was Ola Ragland. She had spent almost all her life teaching there. She was tough, but also fair. About fifteen years ago, I took my children by her house and was surprised to find she was still alive. She remembered me very well. She didn't say it, but I'm sure she was thinking, how could she possibly forget the worst student she ever had?

I'm going to go back when they complete the renovation of the old school. Off to the side of the school stands a cluster of pine trees. The principal asked me if it was true the outdoor bathrooms used to be where the pine trees now stood. Yes, I said, those trees showed up shortly after the bathrooms were torn down.

2006-2007
Seven People and a Corner Table

It wasn't important why they met, for each one would say his piece during the two hours or so while they sat in a corner of McDonalds. Very seldom did any of these men intend to eat. It was a coffee break from all the normal things in life. The discussions ran deep into the problems that faced our country – from war in Iraq, to the sorry state of the United Nations, to any current situations. If that wasn't pressing enough, we relived our lives and how much tougher things were in the late Thirties and Forties. Sometimes I thought, *how could they have had it as bad as me.*

There was one lady among us — she was from China. She spoke four languages, and was an extremely cordial person, but usually kept her stories to herself. Homer, from Beaumont, Texas, had not lost any of his Texas twang and like all Texans, started his stories with "Well, let me tell you about when I was a boy," or something of that nature. He left Texas for Florida, but for some reason, I believe he's still a Texan at heart. Merle was born in Metz, Missouri. He was the facts man of the group. "I don't know about that," he would say. "I'll have to check that out."

Ted was from New York, NY. He was probably the elder statesman of this group. He was one funny man, and loved to laugh.

He was genuine in every respect. One day, he brought in all his World War II memorabilia. They were in a plastic bag: chevrons, longevity hash marks, dog tags, a medal and few other items. He set there pulling out each item, one by one. You could see the look in his eyes as we looked at each keepsake. They don't make people like this any more. He's the last of a dying breed. It's a shame there's very few like him left.

Vaughn was born in Monmouth, Illinois. He had served in the US Air Force during Vietnam. I never could tell if he knew a little about almost any subject; it certainly seemed that way. One thing about him, we had a lot of discussions about many things and yes, I guess you could say he taught me several things, but maybe he borrowed a little bit of knowledge from each of the men who sat at the table in Mickey D's.

Bill was born in Angetown, North Carolina. With all his vast knowledge of the Bible, he should have been a missionary, but then, I guess his mission in life was to spread his good humor among all people. This does not mean that he wouldn't take a stand against anything he felt was wrong. He could be very firm and resolute. He knew well there was good and bad everywhere and yes, Bill loved to smile, and that's the way life should be. As he always says, "The Bible says so and so and that's what I believe."

Al was born in Michigan, a place called Kalkaska. I could write he was a

Democrat and maybe stop there. But the truth is, he's a good man. He's the type of person who if you pull a trick on him, might not even recognize what you said or did. I guess you could say he ignored what he didn't want to hear. He, I'm sure, thought some of us were nuts.

I guess you could say they are all good people and they have made life just a little bit better for each other for we only pass by once and life is forever fleeting.

First at The Table

In the late Thirties, it was a custom in many homes for the adults to eat first, especially if company was present. This was not a form of punishment; it was, plain and simple, a custom in some parts of the Deep South. It did lend to some very empty stomachs, especially if the company was a preacher man with a big appetite. You were very lucky sometimes to have a chicken wing left to eat. If you don't believe this could cause a problem, try sharing a couple chicken wings with four boys!

Many times, only two or three biscuits were left and very little gravy. This could lead to us kids going to bed with empty stomachs. I remember very well when I reached "first at the table" status. But would you believe it, the year I moved up to this lofty status, for some reason we all started to eat together. The rules had changed, or maybe it was because we had all reached an age when we now had proper table manners.

Many people would think this was cruel today, and maybe it was a little unusual. But, one thing I will tell you, with rules like this, home discipline was not a problem.

My Friend Larry — 2005-2007

His name was Larry Clem. It was easy to become friends with him. He was an easy-going person, not pushy in any way. We were both Alabama football fans. We bled crimson from head to toe. When we first started to talk about our lives, it was apparent our backgrounds were similar, although I was born in Alabama and he was born in Jacksonville, Florida. Larry married Becky. She was born in Jasper, Alabama. They have three sons, Scott, David and Wade. Becky is a wonderful wife for Larry and is deeply religious; she is a good and gracious person in all respects.

Larry's mom, Ruth, was born in Greenwood, South Carolina. She is now 82 years old, but she certainly doesn't look that old. Larry and his sister Rhonda love their mom very much. Larry's dad, William (Bill) was also born in Greenwood, South Carolina. He spent 20 years in the Navy, and served in the Pacific theater during World War II. He was loved deeply by Larry. He died in the last year. I only met him once, but he was one good man. They say the good die young, and he certainly proved that to be true. Rhonda was the girl in the family. Looks like her mom, and hasn't aged at all. She and her husband, Fred, have a daughter Courtney and a son, Brad. They are both in their early twenties. I guess you could say Larry has a real good family, but best of all he's my friend.

The Guy Next Door

"Good morning Leo. How's it going?"

"Okay, I guess", he answered. "I've been a little off-color for a few days."

I really suspected nothing wrong but it was a little unusual for Leo to complain about anything. We had lived next door to each other for thirty years. I had watched his three kids grow up, get married and then start their own families. Their names were Leo Jr., Michelle and Sheila. They had been good kids and had now become real good adults. Leo and his wife Dorena had a right to be proud. Our family, four girls and a boy were older than their children, except Billy Jr., who was still at home until he married.

That morning, as I was talking to Leo he mentioned he would be going on a trip with his Model-A club. "Look after the house," he said. We always told each other when we were going to be gone overnight or at vacation times. They were leaving the next morning. He became sick that night and went to the emergency room at Orange Park Medical Center, but after discussing how he felt, they decided to leave on their trip the next morning.

I did not know he had become sick. Later, I learned he had become much worse. They had stopped at a small hospital in Georgia. They, in turn, had transferred him to Emery Hospital in Atlanta. After a week there, they let him transfer to Orange Park in Florida. He was first diagnosed with meningitis and kept in isolation; then they decided he had something else.

I didn't want to expose myself or my family to some unknown disease. Never suspecting this was a fatal condition, I never saw Leo again. He died suddenly. His daughter Michelle stood in our living room, and when she said Leo had died, it hit us all like a bolt of lightening. We were all taken aback. For days and weeks later, when I looked across the fence that separated our homes, I expected to see him smiling back at me. It is so hard to believe he's not still there. He was much more than a neighbor, and I will not forget him. The guy next door was a tremendous person, but even more than that, he was my friend.

England, My England

If for no other reason than its pure beauty, I will never forget my years spent there from the Mersey River that flows through the outer banks and along the docks of Liverpool. I remember well the ferry rides I had from Liverpool to Birkenhead and back. It was a time of my life when I had come to know there was a really big world to see.

The small villages with the whitewashed buildings and their thatched roofs — I just knew this was the height of beauty, on the road to the base where I was stationed. As we crossed into Wales, I could see the mountains starting to rise. If you drove on past the base it wasn't far to Conway, and there a beautiful castle sat near the water on a small hill overlooking the town. The bridge that crossed over the waterway was magnificent.

Oh, yes, I traveled to many other places with wondrous beauty, but they're too numerous for me to mention their names. I am so thankful that I was able to see the beauty of this land. But most of all, my children walked this land with me. Is there anything greater than that which I've mentioned?? Yes, I can assure you, for it was here I first met my Kathleen.

Our Dogs

She was the first dog we ever owned. I brought her home as a puppy in 1964. She was a beautiful collie, with all the looks of Lassie. The children loved her greatly and she returned their love ten-fold. Wherever they were, there you would find Lady. We only had her a few years. One year, we went home to Alabama. She naturally went along. She became sick, and while we were visiting my brother, Herman, he begged us to leave her with him. We decided to leave her because she was losing weight and appeared ill. Herman took her to a veterinarian and then nursed her back to health. She became his constant companion for years. We saw her several times in later times. He had taught her several tricks. She was one smart dog.

Not long after giving Lady to Herman, the kids got a little black and white dog that they named Bandit because he had a white ring around one eye. A bandit he was. He naturally loved the kids, but for some reason his personality changed, and after he bit a little girl on the bum, we were forced to give him away to a farmer.

After Bandit came a great dog, Buffy. I remember going to get her when she was just a little ball of black and fluff. I placed her inside my shirt, and she stuck her head out between the buttons. We should have known just how wonderful she would be from day one. She had this great love for everyone, and her greatest love was for the kids. That first year, I remember her playing in the snow with them; she would bound over the snow banks, sometimes disappearing into the fluffy snow. We didn't know it then, but we would have her for fifteen years. Her love for our kids was total and their love for her was the same.

After we moved to Orange Park, Florida in 1976, Buffy would become friends with our grandson, Christian, a few years later. She was always near Kathleen, and she loved her very much. Buffy was very intelligent, and seemed to understand almost everything we said. Towards the end of her life, she started to go blind, then her kidneys started to fail. She was buried in our backyard beneath a rose bush. Our Buffy had been the best.

When Buffy had pups in South Dakota, Debby selected one puppy as her favorite. When people came to select one of the thirteen puppies, Debby would hide this one puppy. When all the pups were gone, except this little reddish-gold and white puppy, it was declared she would stay with us. Debbie named her Becky-Sue. Aside from being very fast, she was a great Frisbee player. She was entered in the mutt races at Rapid City dog track and never lost. Donna was the official come-to-me Becky person during the races. Becky-Sue, like her mom, was very smart and loved everyone. When we came to Orange Park, she disappeared one day, and was never seen again.

Before we left South Dakota, Becky had puppies and from this litter came Luke. He was much larger than his mom. He was a truly loveable dog, but when he was less than a year old, he went outside one night. When he came inside, he walked in front of me, then he stopped. He had this strange look on his face. I reached out to touch him, and he fell over, dead. We never knew what happened to him.

A few years after Buffy died, Donna came to our house one day and said, "I've found the perfect dog for you and mom. A family is moving. They have this beautiful black cocker spaniel. He is not even a year old." We first said "no". Then, "maybe". She brought him to our house. He was beautiful, and so started the years of Sammy.

That night he followed us to the bedroom. He sat on the floor looking at us. His beautiful eyes and red tongue were visible in the partially lit room. Kath's first words were, "No dog is going to sleep on my bed." Sammy just sat there looking at us. Finally Kath looked at him. He was so pathetic. She said, "Okay." He lunged onto the bed and curled up in a ball at our feet. It took him all of the next morning to work his way up between us.

Sammy was a strong little dog. You never took him for a walk — he took you. He would literally pull you along. His real name was Tommy's Mr. Samson and he was strong. One day, Billy asked if we would keep his bassett hound Dudley for a while. A few years later, he was still with us. He was a great dog. He had a lot less loose skin than normal, but was also light-colored. His hair was like yellow sand, but he also had white around his neck and chest. Like I said, he was beautiful. Sammy was notorious at running away. He took Dudley on many runs for miles, one time all the way to Middleburg.

One year, Billy was babysitting the dogs while we went to England. They got out and were gone for several days. When they were finally found, a car had hit Sammy on River Road. He was dead, and lying on top of him was Dudley. No one could come near. We had Dudley for a few more years. Then one day, in the yard, he jumped off a piece of plywood, and did something to his neck. He had torn vertebrae in his neck; nothing could help him. He was put to sleep. It was like losing a member of the family. The saga of the dogs we had and loved was over. Only the memories remain.

The Lives of War Hawk Bird That Flies (Fiction)

His name was David Goodland, but as was the custom when he reached two years old, his Indian name would be given to him during a tribal council meeting. That name was War Hawk Bird That Flies. His father would not know that day what he would grow to become. David went to tribal school like all the other children born on this reservation in South Dakota. He was very smart, and received the highest marks for his leadership qualities.

As he grew over the years, he did anything his mom and dad asked. They were very proud of him. When he reached eighteen years old, he went to his first dance, and at this dance he was introduced to what the Indians called fire water. The year was 1944.

Meanwhile, at the white man's college in Colorado, a group of scientists had started to experiment with a time machine they had built. This was kept very secret from anyone connected to the university. Their idea was to in some way rescue someone at the instant when their body and brain would be at the dividing point between life and death, and place this person in their time machine.

Then, they could study this person who was neither dead nor alive. They could, by flipping a switch, move him milliseconds on either side of death or life. They studied him in thousands of ways; always with the thought that they would eventually figure out how to control life and death.

The scientists waited until a public execution was to take place. They did not have to wait long. That year, David Goodland, a.k.a. War Hawk Bird That Flies, started to drink booze heavily. One night, at the height of a drunken stupor, he killed a man. His mom and dad were devastated. He was tried, and sentenced to be hanged on his nineteenth birthday, December 21, 1944. He was to be hung a half-mile out of town out on the prairie. The scientists took two vehicles: one loaded with explosives, would remain on the opposite side of town, while the other with the time machine, would attend the hanging and rescue the hanged man. At the moment the trap door on the scaffold was sprung, the explosions were set off. All the people rushed to the town. The scientists rushed David's body to the time machine. They turned it on and took him back in time twelve hours. He sat up as though he had only been asleep.

When they arrived back in Colorado, they took him to their laboratory and the experiments began. They would observe his actions, vital signs and his ability to live and do all normal things a young man could do. He would become agitated at times, but normally was calm.

But one night in 1955, after all this time going in and out of the time machine and looking at all the test equipment in the lab, he managed to escape. He was amazed when he walked down a street. He had never seen neon lights before. He looked for any place he recognized, but saw nothing.

Finally, he walked into a bar. He asked for a drink, and then sat down at a table. When he looked up in a corner of the bar, something he had never seen before caught his eye. A television was showing an old movie. Indians were attacking a house in the Old West. A cowboy came around the side of a cabin, and was walking straight at an Indian, with his large revolver pointed straight out through the TV screen at David. That's when he leaped to his feet, grabbed a chair and destroyed the TV.

He ran down the street, back to the laboratory, sat down in the time machine, and set the dial to full return. Instantly, he found himself hanging from a rope and falling through a trap door. He could feel someone cutting the rope. He fell to the ground below. He sat there for a few moments, then reached up and removed the rope from his neck.

He walked back into town, then into the town saloon. He walked up to the bar and ordered a drink. There was no response form the bartender. He did sit a drink on the counter near him, but probably for the man who stood by him. He reached for the drink, but his hand passed through the glass. War Hawk Bird That Flies walked outside. In the distance, he could hear the coyote's lonesome cry, and the far-off ancient drumbeat of life. He knew now he could never return to the life he once knew.

The Day Our Church Was Stolen

For years, we had heard of the changes that were coming in the Episcopal Church. Most cradle Episcopalians thought this was just another rumor. But one day in New Hampshire, a priest who had left his wife and children and was living openly with his male partner, became the Bishop of New Hampshire. This would trigger a movement of liberalism throughout the church. The storm clouds were no longer gathering. The storm had arrived.

Within one year, the Scriptures were being challenged in every way. Jesus was said to not be the only way into heaven. Sin was no longer sin. The Scriptures were old and outdated — a more progressive approach to Christianity was just on the horizon. The northern Diocese of Florida had elected a new bishop.

A short while before this started, we thought no way would he be a part of this ungodly alliance, but we didn't take into consideration that he was a lawyer before he became a bishop. When he threw himself in with this lot, a slight tremor could be felt in some of the churches, including our own. It would soon grow to righteous indignation. Then, finally, a complete split with the Episcopal Church.

So was born a place of worship named The Church of the Good Samaritan (Anglican). This would raise the question, will we retain the church and its property? After all, the Diocese had paid nothing toward purchase of the land or building of the church. There was another matter. If the Diocese had decided to no longer honor Bible teaching, on which our church was based, then the Diocese had broken its communion with our congregation. While we admit that legally (by Florida law) the Diocese holds the deed to our church, it is only that way because they would not recognize any church unless they held the deed to its property.

To say that our church and property has been stolen from us may sound harsh. But in plain language, when you take something from someone that they worked for, and then purchased, that's thievery — period! As for those who do not believe this to be true, let them argue this on the Day of Judgment before our God. They may find their law degrees a little lacking on that day.

Letter To My Friend

Dear Don,

Thought I might touch base with you, as it's been a while since we last talked. I know the postage will be pretty expensive, with this letter having to travel so far, but that's okay, friend. I'll pay this time. I'm sure you're playing a lot of golf. Did you ever cure that slice? Probably not. I haven't played lately. Legs just won't carry me around like they used to.

Most of the courses here are suffering from lack of rain. It's been one dry spring. I'm sure the weather is much better there. I'll bet you have to be real honest about what you make on each hole. Wouldn't do any good to lie. The man probably has instant replay. By the way, have you beat him yet? I understand you can drive a ball for miles there. Wouldn't do any good to tee it high like they say, and watch it fly. You could use a nine iron and hit it out of sight.

By the way how's the wine? It should be great, especially with him changing the water into whatever you would like. Oh yeah, I forgot to ask if he plays well. I wouldn't advise you trying to give him lessons. You'll have to remember he's probably played with some of the best, ever.

Well, friend, I know you must be enjoying yourself. I'm sure I'll join you before too long. By the way, should I bring my clubs? Well, Don, that's about it. Oh yeah, almost forgot, Gloria is doing good. Of course she misses you. We talk about you at times. Jim and Cindy are doing great. So is Linda and her family. I'm sure you know your grandchildren are growing up. I would say all the best but you've got that already. I talk to

Jesus pretty regularly. You know that way you get preferred tee times. Later. That's about it.

Until,

Bill

Wet Birds Do Not Fly At Night

The first time I heard the story "wet birds do not fly at night" was in South Dakota, when I was stationed at Ellsworth AFB. For the life of me, I cannot remember who told me this bizarre story. Anyway, one morning a few years after I first hear it, when arriving at the Alert Force Bombing Compound where I was the maintenance supervisor, I found the flight chief for that shift had been awake all night. One of the B-52's bombing radar was broken; this was causing some major problems for the Strategic Air Command, as a major target was not covered if we went to war. Now, even though this flight chief could do nothing to fix this plane, nevertheless, he was responsible. The pressure on him was very severe and it had lasted all night. Trying to relieve some of this pressure, I proceeded to tell him this story.

"One day a man woke up, and after dressing, stepped outside his home. It was a beautiful day, unlike any he could remember. The sky was a beautiful blue, but much more blue than he had ever seen it before. The trees and grass were more beautiful than he had ever noticed. When he saw and listened to the birds, they were more beautiful and sang with great splendor. He thought, *how can our world be so perfect?*

Over the next few weeks, he asked several people if this had happened to them. Some responded with a sort of "yes" but most were not sure.

Finally, one night while having a drink in a bar, he struck up a conversation with a man. As they talked, this man told him he had heard of a wise man in the Himalayan Mountains who could give him the answer to all his questions in just a few words. With this promise of maybe finally answering or resolving his question about all he had seen and felt that wonderful morning, he proceeded to work and save up his money for five years.

One day, he was finally ready to depart for the Himalaya Mountains. Arriving there, he hired four people to carry all his supplies and climbing equipment. They struck out on the climb to the top of these mountains during the very best of weather. Two weeks later, he awoke one morning and all the people assisting him were gone. He was now all alone, but desperate to succeed. He took what he could carry, and proceeded to continue the climb. After several weeks, he had run out of food, his clothes were in shreds and he had many cuts on his body from the jagged rocks. He was nearing death, but still he pressed on.

Late one afternoon, he topped a very high peak. He lay down; then, looking over, he saw a valley, with a small street paved of pure gold, jutting out of the mountain. He now crawled on his hands and knees toward a temple. He could see a head as he reached the top of some giant steps; he now looked down a hallway. He could see, seated on a throne, an old man with a long beard. He crawled to the feet of the old man. As he lay there, he knew he was dying, but as his final act he wanted to know what he had traveled all this way for.

He now spoke, "Oh wise man, what is the meaning of the earth, the sky, the animals, the birds and all the beauty around us? But most of all, what is the meaning of *me*?" The wise man looked down on this pitiful man then said, " Wet birds do not fly at night." The beaten man then asked, "Oh wise man, what do you mean wet birds do not fly at night?" The old man then said, "You mean, they *do*?"

Sorry I had to do this to you, but what the heck...paper is cheap.

The Song "Old Blue"

The first time I heard this little song, my Mom was humming it in the kitchen in Coaldale. I was about seven or eight years old. She told me it had been passed down through her family, and she had learned the words while traveling in a covered wagon across Kansas in the year 1908. Her father sang it at night around the campfire. She said every one would join in. Soon all the kids knew every word in the song and this was what they learned:

I had a little dog, and his name was Blue
And I'll sing to you what he would do,
He would leave the house right after dark
And down in the hollow you could hear him
*   bark.*
I would go down there; see what he had
*   treed*
He'd have a possum up a white oak tree.
I'd take my hand and pull him down
I said, "Old Blue, we'll bake him brown."
Now Blue took sick, so very sick
I sent for the doctor and said, "Come quick!"
The doctor came and he came in a run
He said, "Old Blue, your hunting's done."
Old Blue he died, he died so hard,
He shook holes in our front yard.
We buried him in a shady place
And covered him over with a possum's face.

*Now when I die, I know what I'll do,
I'll go to heaven and call for Blue.*

When Mom died in 1990, a little girl, a relative of mine, was swinging in my sister's yard. We had come there for my mom's funeral. I said to the young girl, "I'll sing you a song you've never heard." As I sang this song, I had gone about half way through it, when all at once she started to sing it along with me. I knew then this song would never die. A few years later, our grandchildren would start to sing Old Blue with me: Rachel, Sarah, Jordan and Megan would pick up the song easily. It has, and will always remain, important that this song be passed to generations to come. Some things were meant to remain and this song is one of those that is supposed to be never forgotten.

To Those Who Cannot Laugh And Smile

As I write this, I honestly believe I would not be alive if my personality had been such that I could not smile and laugh during some terrible times and conditions. Many times in my life, I have been asked, "How can you laugh when something very serious was happening, or about to happen?" My answer to that might not be appropriate at the time, but it is straight from the heart: To mope and moan about a bad situation resolves nothing, and in fact, will probably make things far worse.

One year in South Dakota at the Air Force base where I was stationed, a B-52 crashed; after a daring rescue, the fire department managed to save the crew. All crewmembers except one were not injured, and the one who was hurt was fine after surgery on his leg. I was on the investigation team looking into the accident; finding a rat that had drowned in fuel in a pump house, I placed a red investigation tag around his neck. I then told one of the officers in charge there was a casualty in the pump house, and finding the rat, he exploded.

I started to laugh, and he could not understand how I could laugh during this investigation. I looked at him. All the people on board the aircraft had survived. It was unbelievable.

"What was in order?" I asked him. "We don't cry for machinery, and the plane could and would be replaced. I know it's hard for some people to smile and laugh. Some were put on this earth so they could make a decision, smile a lot, laugh a lot or cry a lot. That's your choice", I said. "I'll take the laughs and smiles. If you can't do that, then accept your misery, but don't complain. I'm just too busy counting my blessings and smiling."

The Flag

For two hundred years and more, no one has questioned what our flag has stood for. When George Washington led our men across the Delaware River, the flag went with the first boat.

Later on, it would fly in many battles. It was a standard that stood for "Here we are, defeat us if you can!" Later it would be carried into the worst war this country ever experienced as brother fought brother, North against South. When it all ended, Old Glory was still standing proud. This flag was carried at the forefront of many campaigns. It was as though as long as it stood, defeat was impossible.

During WWI, it was carried through the Meuse-Argonne while many thousands died. When the charge from the trenches came, the flag was always out in front of the troops.

My dad, who fought in all the major battles in France during WWI, said, "As long as you could see the Stars and Stripes out front, you knew you were winning."

During WWII, throughout some of the most brutal battles ever fought, the flag was presented for all to see. Today it is featured as a symbol of our stand for freedom in most of the monuments throughout Washington D.C. In Korea, even as the enemy overpowered our troops with enormous manpower, the flag still waved over all the battles. In Vietnam, it was displayed on anything that was used to fight with. even on uniforms and caps. The flag would not go, no matter what, but in the late 1960's, a new breed of American appeared.

They draped themselves in American flags and declared, "peace at any cost". They burned Old Glory. As they did this in public, our enemies seeing this, realized that these were not the Americans of yesteryear, so Old Glory was stomped and burned in the streets. They even declared themselves patriots.

When all was lost, a generation of new men and women stepped forward. They brought with them love of country, love of ideals, and most of all, love of freedom. Old Glory was back as a symbol of greatness.

The Iron Men And The Sea

When Kathleen and I returned to England in the fall of 2007, we were blessed with beautiful, clear but also cool weather. I went to some horse racing at a place called Ludlow, and also at Pontrefact, Wolverhamptom, and the Grand National Course at Aintree.

In the year 2005, a designer of unusual sculptures placed 100 cast iron figures of himself on the shoreline from Blundell Sands to Seaforth, England, which is an approximate distance of two miles. There was no set pattern; some were placed about one mile out from the beach and when the tide went out (about two miles), then all of these figures would become visible.

Some were placed nearer the shore, and as you walk along the beach, they tower above you, all facing towards the Irish Sea. As you stand there looking at them, a feeling of awe surrounds you. It's as though you are looking at an awesome display of a man's inner feeling. It is a display like none you've seen before. The figures are nine feet tall and become completely exposed when the tide is fully out (and I do mean *exposed*, as they are nude). They completely disappear at high tide—gradually disappearing, until only the waves surge past them.

The man who made these sculptures of himself, Anthony Gromley, placed them here with an initial plan to remove them later for shipment to the U.S., but the people who lived in this borough liked them so much, they could not see them leaving. They raised enough money to purchase them from Anthony Gromley. So here they will stay—100 iron men forever facing toward the Irish Sea.

Kath and I visited her brother Gegs and his wife Lily who lived in Formby village and then went and stayed awhile with her other brother, Jim and his wife Lorna. It was strange as we drove along the streets of Liverpool. I was 18 years old when I first came here. It was another lifetime ago and a lot has changed in this old sea town. But a lot has also remained as it was a hundred years ago. The ferry across the Mersey, made famous by the singing group "Jerry and the Pacemakers", still runs to Birkenhead. I rode it many times to meet my Kathleen in the early 1950s. Yes, I have many memories and all of them a wonderful time of my life.

The Letter

She was always a very smart little girl, but I don't think anyone realized the feelings she had for her fellow man. When she wrote this letter in November of 2007, it came as a shock how caring and intelligent she is, but I guess we should have known she would inherit these traits from her mother, Julie and her dad, Jim. To them I say, you have raised a terrific little girl. This is what she wrote, so that we might share in her feelings:

Dear Brave Soldier:

I can't imagine how I would feel if you were my daddy. My heart would ache, for I love him so much, tears would burst from my eyes like a tumbling water fall, smashing and crashing against an old stone cliff. I sit quietly and think of you out there and how your family must feel without you. I know you miss them.

Without you, evil people may take over the world as we know it. You're there to defend our country and I understand that now. I never used to understand the meaning of war, but now that I'm a little older and more mature, I've developed a passion for peace and joy. I'm praying my twin brothers or my Daddy don't have to go to war some day. Lately, I have been affected by the dreadful things on TV, always hoping for wars to finally end. I heard about people being shot or bombs and many other things. It sounds horrid and especially sad. I wouldn't have wanted you to experience anything so dreadful.

I wrote my biography project about John McCrae and his poem, which he wrote during the war. His poem, "Flanders' Fields" was the start of the Poppy symbol to remember brave soldiers in battle. I got to read the poem in assembly, it really touched my heart. I am so proud of it, as I'm proud of you, always wondering how frightening and how terribly horrid it must be, either losing someone close or something precious.

You're so brave, strong, loyal and honourable. I'm counting on you to do your best, and to try your hardest to do good, risking being hurt or even your life for our country is so brave. I want a good future with a husband and children, as do many others like my friends. There's many more exciting things to come yet. Let us live them. Remember you will always be in my thoughts, and thank you.

From

Marie-Claire Rose Smith.
11 years old

Love To All – February 17, 2006

It is now spring, 2006. Kathy and I have lived here in Florida since 1977. We have watched our children grow up, marry and give to us tremendous happiness. Through all our grandchildren, we have so much to be thankful for. What a great life we have and share with each other! Kath is now 72 years old and I am 74. When we met, I was 19 and she was 17. It has been a long and beautiful trip, with just a few bumps in the road. Few are as blessed as we are, and for that we give thanks.

As I write this last chapter, I sincerely hope you have enjoyed what I have written for you. I leave you with these thoughts: Life comes full circle. As our mothers and fathers before us, we have raised our children. Now they do the same. Kathleen and I have laughed, loved, and lived a wonderful life. We pass this on to those that follow. I hope they find the same happiness we did, after all, what else is there?

Beside The Road

The little flower that sits by the road
From season to season it comes and it goes.

I stopped one day to take a look
Its petals were like an open book.

Its face so beautiful and full of glee
I wondered what it was thinking of me.

On my way home late at night
With all life's problems things never seem
right.

I looked outside and what would I see
That same little flower looking back at me.

I stopped there looking with dismay
For when winter comes it goes away.

But then spring returns with warmth and light
The little flower burst forth with all of its might

Back again to cheer us all
That little flower so very small.

Waving and smiling for you and for me
Beside the road it will always be.

Billy Jack Marsh
April 8, 1990

Santa's Ride

The year was nineteen-eighty-five
And Santa was ready to make his ride
His first stop was in the black hills land
To see Andrea, Judy and Dan.
And after staying a little while,
"Have to leave folks must travel many
a mile,"
And with unfinished business he sprang
to his sleigh
"On Donner and Blitzen," you could
hear him say.
Down from the North he roared with a
flash
To see all the people that had spent all
their cash
He made all his rounds from this house
to that
This jolly old fellow so round and so fat
He stopped at Middleburg and
Orange Park too
For everyone seemed to be in a bit of
a stew
"Did I buy everything?" people will say
"And most of all, will I be able to pay?"
Then slowly they realize it's not what
you pay

That makes this a wonderful Christmas
Day,
It's just being together and sitting
around
Watching each other's happiness
abound.
Now after Santa's chores are all done,
He will declare, "It's been a great lot of
fun."
Now from the rooftops he gave a loud
shout—
"Isn't that what Christmas is all about?"
He roared back North over I-95
Homeward bound he did fly
But off in the distance you could hear
one last cheer,
"Merry Christmas to all, I'll see you next
year!"

The "Dream" I Had Last Night

This was the dream I had one night
My heart filled with anguish, my soul
filled with fright.

I stood on a street as a man walked
by,
My eyes welled with tears that I could
not hide.
I was in a town so far away,
I looked at his face and I heard
someone say,
"It must be Jesus for lo and behold
Angels walked with Him, through this
street very old."

On this street stood a lady dressed in
white,
I knew as I saw her – she like me full of
fright.
She looked at Him then softly said,
"Are you the Messiah of which I have
read?

They said one day you would finally
come here."
He smiled, reached out to brush away
her tears.

Then I heard Him say, "I am Jesus, I've
come back again
To gather all people who would stand
against sin.

So if you love Me and would live life
this way
Then arise and follow, as I go on my
way."

The synagogues were closed as word
had now spread,
He had returned, just as His disciples
had said.
Rabbis walked these streets with
bowed heads,
Then Jesus looked at them, and this is
what He said.

"You are my people, the chosen ones.
Will you now follow me? For I am
God's Son."

Finally we came to this holy place,
Where we were to receive our
judgment or grace.
The lines formed long for many miles.
Then finally I looked into His eyes.

I knelt before Him there that day, to
receive my judgment,
Now what would He say?
Suddenly I awoke from my dream,
All my life had passed it seemed.

I had met my God and heard Him say,
"Well done, my son, come home with
me today."

Then as I turned to walk away, one last
thing I heard Him say,
"I've heard your poems," He said to
me, "written by your hand to glorify
me."

Now if you have a dream like I had
that day
I hope you can feel as I do today.
If not, there's still time to kneel down
and pray.
May God bless and keep us forever
and today.

Amen

Billy Jack Marsh
August 1993

Because I Chose To Do So

This is a story about this old man who walked without Jesus throughout this great land. He had lived as a sinner for most of his life, while Jesus stood waiting through all of his strife.

-----Because I Chose To Do So-----
When most of his youth was finally done
Only then would he seek out God's only Son

-----Because I Chose To Do So-----
Then one day he went down on his knees
Looked up to God and said help me please
He had done no service for this Holy One
But now he came begging for help from His Son

-----Because I Chose To Do So-----
Now His arms they encircle me tight
The power of His spirit surges through me at night
When dawns light streaks across the sky
He opens his eyes and starts to cry
Oh Heavenly Father, be with me today

Protect and keep me as I go on my
way
     -----Because I Chose To Do So-----
Now when I'm troubled and kneel
down to pray
I look up to heaven I can hear Him say
I am with you and forever will be
Go love one another as you would
love Me
Wherever you go no matter what time
of the day
Remember I'm with you each step of
the way
     -----Because I Chose To Do So-----

The Satellite Dish

This is a story about a satellite dish
To watch Saturday football was all that he
wished
But lo and behold it stuck over a fence
The neighbor next door became very
incensed
The neighbor next door said, "It's got to go"
But the man that put it up there said,
"Definitely no."
The neighbor next door got very mad
And made the man with a dish next door
very sad
He nailed boards together so brassy and bold
And put aluminum foil on the end of the pole
Placing the pole in a strategic place
The dish could pick up nothing, not even a
trace
The police came to sort out this mess
But what could they do, they had to confess
The moral of this story is very plain
People from Liverpool just aren't very sane
How did they solve it, nobody knows
That neighbor next door stepped on our
Geg's toes.

> Billy Jack Marsh
> October 10, 1990

— Blessed —

I look upon the sky so blue
While wisps of clouds come passing through
The sun sits there day after day
And warms our earth with golden rays

Alone at night with all the stars
They seem so close not very far
I gaze upon the Milky Way
While shooting stars come out to play

Sometimes we stand and look on high
As darkened clouds come paint the sky
The rains come forth so very near
To green our earth we love so dear

How could this wondrous beauty be,
Without God's love for you and me?

> Billy Jack Marsh
> August, 1975 – Utapao, Thailand

Gus Lives On

Born into poverty
This old man
For sixty-one years
He walked this land

In World War I he heard the call
In the Battle of The Argonne he stood very tall

He met my mom in Twenty Three
And soon there was this family

He labored hard all his life
To feed his family and his wife

We didn't have much during all those years
Many times I saw his eyes full of tears

In Nineteen Fifty when war came
I said, "You served, I'll do the same"

He shook my hand; we said goodbye
Then six weeks later, he would die

I remember well his wrinkled face
As age came forth and took his place

The spring from his walk had disappeared
I should have known the end was near

Up US Thirty One there is a town
Where we laid my old dad down

Now if you should happen by
Just give a wave and tell him Hi

If he was here this very day
I wonder what he would have to say

He would probably say what a crowd
And I want you to know I'm very proud

Now he's gone, he did not die
He simply waved and said goodbye

Somewhere out there he waits for us all,
My old Dad the best of them all

His spirit now lives within my eyes
Old Gus, you see, will never die.

June 26, 1990

Billy Jack Marsh

Ode To Eliza Jane

For ninety years
She lived her life
With all her love
She knew no strife

Jesus called, she went away
Her victory won this very day

The sting of death is no more
She left here like a closing door

Now she walks in the sun
Her work on earth she knows is done
Now just look around, you all will see
The very best of her legacy

I knew her well, they all will say
As we stood around this sorrowful day

Now she's there amongst the stars
Looking down from afar

Waiting and watching for a familiar face
Saying, welcome to this beautiful place.

April 3, 1990

Mother's Day

I met her in Nineteen Fifty One
To a foreign land I had come

I married her in Waterloo
She was the loveliest girl I ever knew

Five children came in the next eight years
Her heart was filled with joy and cheer

I wonder sometimes if children know
How deep a mother's love does go

So on this, your Mother's Day
This is what I want to say

I just wanted you to know
That though I married you long ago

It seems like yesterday to me,
So thanks a bunch for marrying me

I love you more than words can say,
So all the best, on this your day.

All My Love Always

May 13, 1990

Ode to Old B-52

O Great Bird that flies so high
And looks so graceful in the sky
Who did its mission great or small
Who made SACs men look so very tall.

She came to this land so far away
And for eight years she would stay
For most of these years she would fight
While Charlie cringed in desperate fright

The men would call her a hulk of rust
And look at her with great disgust
She would sit there with no fear
For she knew she had no peer.

To many she was known as the Old Black Buff
All her life she was treated rough
The men who worked on this bird of prey
Would never know an eight-hour day.

Although they called her many names
Old B-52 remained the same
Although not a plane of beauty
She knew how to do her duty

For many years, TAC had their show
Now it was time for SAC to have a go
So it was in '72
That we launched the B-52s

Movies, Giant Cookies & a Panther

She was equal to the task
And North Vietnam felt her vengeful blast
Their streets in ruins, their buildings alight
To the peace tables they went, to make
things right

Now it was in '75
That Old B-52 would homeward fly
Her work well done, she bears no shame
The decisions made were not her blame

Charlie rose and gave a cheer
For the Old B-52 was leaving here
But as you know, and I do too,
This is not the end of Old B-52

For she's always there, just one flight away
To come again, and save the day.

Bill Marsh
Utapao, Thailand
June 8, 1975

243

Billy Jack Marsh

Ode to Good Sams

This little ole church that sit by the road,
where people gather to surrender their souls

In this church you will find many things, priests
and acolytes and a choir that sure sings

There's Roy with his warm friendly grin,
preaching the virtues of life without sin

There's Barbara who stands so bold, singing
her hymns and touching our souls

There once was Joe with his beard and hair
streaked with gray red socks and all reading
Timothy each day

Then there's Father Hunt the young cavalier
preaching the gospel with hope and good
cheer

There's Friar Tuck (he knows who I mean) with
his great white robe fit for a king

All manner people come to this church they
say but they all look the same when they
kneel down to pray

There's Helen, Barbara, Missy, Puchi, Sharon,
Warren, Carol, Ed, Charlene, and my
Kathleen, the most wonderful people that
I've ever seen

If in this poem I left out your name, please
remember, dear friends, that I love you the
same

Now you've heard this poem, there's little
else to say, so won't you take a moment
please, and bow your head and pray:

Oh Heavenly Father, the maker of man, the
King of this universe and this beautiful land;
You who walk with us each day and kneel
beside us while we pray, when all our worldly
works are done, please take us home, Father,
to be with your Son.
Amen

Billy Jack Marsh April 9, 1993

I Just Thought You Would Want to Know

Several thousand years ago
There was a man who walked this land
He built the earth for all to see
A beautiful place you must agree

Then it was time to make a man
This he accomplished with the wave of his
hand
You must be perfect he said, just like me
Tall and straight like a giant oak tree
Intelligent and witty a smile on his face
The very best of the human race

Now what could he name this marvelous
man
Who would own and populate this wonderful
land
He thought of many letters to make up a
name
Then this thought came racing straight to his
brain

M for Masterful
A for Articulate
R for Rarity
S for Studious
H for Handsome

A name so great for all to see
The greatest name that would ever be

So to all the others that walk this land
Be proud to shake a Marsh's hand

We came here the chosen few,
But of this I'm sure you already knew

Some will marry and think their name is gone
But if you look deep within yourself
You'll find the name goes on.

Did this happen? I really don't know,
But if it didn't, it should have so long ago.

I guess by now you'll all agree
To be a Marsh is great, you see,
So look out world, we all want to say—
The Marshes are here
And here we will stay.

March 1990

Billy Jack Marsh

Movies, Giant Cookies & a Panther

Billy Jack Marsh

www.ingramcontent.com/pod-product-compliance
Lightning Source LLC
Chambersburg PA
CBHW031831090426
42741CB00005B/205